GÉRARD DE NERVAL

suivi de

POÉSIE ET MYSTIQUE

DU MÊME AUTEUR

L'Ame romantique et le Rêve. Essai sur le romantisme allemand et la poésie française. Éditions des *Cahiers du Sud*, Marseille, 1937, deux volumes in-8º (Dépôt à Paris, Librairie José Corti, 6, rue de Clichy).

TRADUCTIONS

A LA LIBRAIRIE STOCK

JEAN-PAUL : *Hespérus*, deux volumes, 1930.

JEAN-PAUL : *Le Jubilé*, 1930 (Cabinet cosmopolite).

JEAN-PAUL : *Choix de rêves*, précédé d'un essai sur Jean-Paul, 1932 (Cabinet cosmopolite).

GŒTHE : *Entretiens avec le Chancelier de Müller*, 1930 (Cabinet cosmopolite).

GŒTHE : *Confessions d'une belle âme*, 1931 (A la Promenade).

KEYSERLING : *Méditations sud-américaines*, 1932.

CHEZ D'AUTRES ÉDITEURS

EDUARD MŒRIKE : *Le Voyage de Mozart*, Préface d'André Cœuroy, Fourcade, 1929.

E. T. A. HOFFMANN : *Salvator Rosa*, Schiffrin, 1926.

E. T. A. HOFFMANN : *Kreisleriana*. Préface d'André Schaeffner. Fourcade, 1931.

LUDWIG TIECK : *La Coupe d'Or et autres contes*. Préface d'Edmond Jaloux. Denoël et Steele, 1933.

ALBERT BÉGUIN

GÉRARD DE NERVAL

suivi de

POÉSIE ET MYSTIQUE

avec une lettre inédite de Nerval

PARIS
LIBRAIRIE STOCK
DELAMAIN ET BOUTELLEAU
7, rue du Vieux-Colombier

POUR RAYMONDE

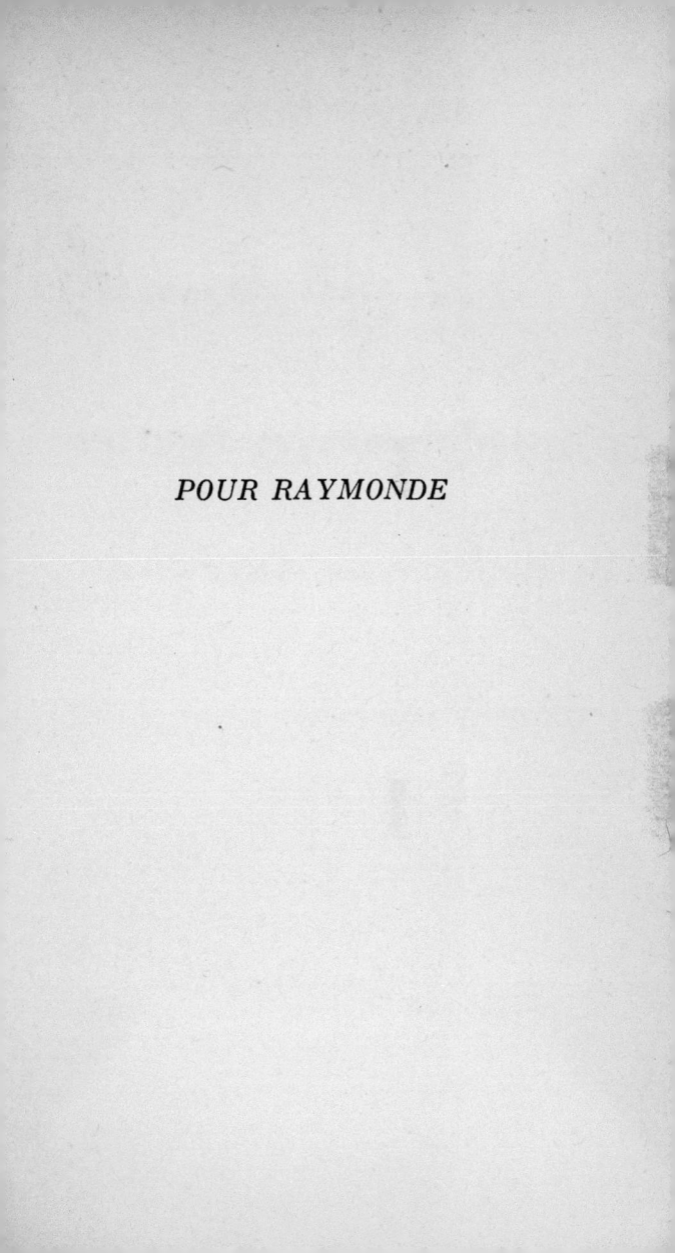

GÉRARD DE NERVAL

ET

LA DESCENTE AUX ENFERS

> « Quoi qu'il en soit, je crois que l'imagination humaine n'a rien inventé qui ne soit vrai, dans ce monde ou dans les autres, et je ne pouvais douter de ce que j'avais *vu* si distinctement. »
>
> *Aurélia.*

De tous les poètes qui se sont aventurés aux frontières de l'abîme, Gérard de Nerval était destiné à être le plus méconnu. Ses amis ont une grande responsabilité dans la naissance de cette légende du « fol délicieux », qui permet de rendre anodin son message, et c'est sous cette gracieuse apparence de farfadet romantique qu'une gloire croissante l'immortalise. Que l'on contemple pourtant l'émouvant visage que présente l'inoubliable photographie de Nadar, authentique chef-d'œuvre de cet art, où se lit une extraordinaire destinée humaine. L'intelligence singulière d'un regard venu de loin, la souffrance que tra-

hissent les deux moitiés si dissemblables
de la face tourmentée, l'humilité digne,
résignée, de toute l'attitude effacent vite
la première impression, qui était d'un
bohème slave, marqué par la misère.

Aux craintifs, qui redoutent de se trouver
face à face avec certaines angoisses, Nerval a donné lui-même les moyens d'atténuer la portée de son œuvre ; sans parler
de ceux qui invoquent, pour le discréditer,
son séjour parmi les fous, on peut relever
dans la correspondance de Gérard et dans
Aurélia assez d'humbles déclarations où
il semble reconnaître l'illusion dont il fut
victime. Ici, comme à propos de Rimbaud, il est facile de faire porter à quelques
phrases bien choisies tout le poids de la
confession, et d'en éviter d'autres, lumineuses mais bien embarrassantes dès qu'on
en accepte loyalement le témoignage. Le
ton de Nerval, qui est l'un des miracles
absolus de la poésie française, favorise ces
erreurs : l'un des combats les plus désespérés
qu'ait livrés l'âme humaine est raconté
avec une absence de pathétique extérieur
et une courtoisie d'expression, qui peuvent

fort bien empêcher que l'on ne sente d'abord tout l'héroïsme de cette exploration de la nuit. Un homme qui se débat contre des fantômes et qui erre dans les ténèbres, éclaire son récit d'une lumière immatérielle. Mais il ne faut pas s'y tromper : cette prose aérienne et délicate traduit une expérience pour laquelle un autre n'eût trouvé que des cris ou des balbutiements éperdus. Jamais pareil équilibre de la forme n'a triomphé d'une aussi furieuse masse de lave ; jamais la légèreté n'a emprisonné dans un aussi fin cristal une réalité lourde de tout le destin des hommes.

Car *Aurélia* est l'histoire d'une lutte titanique, qui s'achève par un triomphe. Triomphe sur quoi ? de quels pouvoirs, à travers ses épreuves et ses visions, cet esprit s'est-il emparé ? quelles certitudes a-t-il conquises ? Quelles sont ces clartés qui, succédant à la nuit et aux cauchemars, illuminent les suprêmes étapes du voyage ?

« Je crois que l'imagination humaine n'a rien inventé qui ne soit vrai, dans ce monde ou dans les autres... », dit Nerval,

sûr d'avoir *vu* des objets réels. Ces lignes
où, sur la foi de son expérience, il affirme
que l'imagination est un moyen de connaissance, et que dès ce monde-ci nous pouvons
communiquer avec quelque autre, font
ressortir toute l'ironie avec laquelle il
parle ailleurs de sa « maladie » et de sa
« guérison ». La célèbre lettre à Mme Dumas,
écrite au sortir de la maison de santé
après la première crise de 1841, ne laisse
place à aucune équivoque.

« J'ai rencontré hier Dumas... Il vous
dira que j'ai recouvré ce que l'on est
convenu d'appeler raison, mais n'en croyez
rien. Je suis et j'ai toujours été le même...
L'illusion, le paradoxe, la présomption
sont toutes choses ennemies du bon sens,
dont je n'ai jamais manqué. Au fond, j'ai
fait un rêve très amusant, et je le regrette ;
j'en suis même à me demander s'il n'était
pas plus *vrai* que ce qui me semble seul
explicable et naturel aujourd'hui. Mais
comme il y a ici des médecins et des commissaires *qui veillent à ce qu'on n'étende pas
le champ de la poésie aux dépens de la voie
publique,* on ne m'a laissé sortir et vaguer

définitivement parmi les gens raisonnables que lorsque je suis convenu bien formellement d'avoir été malade, ce qui coûtait beaucoup à mon amour-propre et même à ma véracité... Pour en finir, je suis convenu de me laisser classer dans une « affection » définie par les docteurs et appelée indifféremment Théomanie ou Démonomanie dans le Dictionnaire médical. A l'aide des définitions incluses dans ces deux articles, la science a le droit d'escamoter ou réduire au silence tous les prophètes et voyants prédits par l'Apocalypse, dont je me flattais d'être l'un !... »

Dans *Aurélia* même, où il dit ne s'être « jamais senti mieux portant » que pendant sa maladie, il se raille des psychiatres qui ont la prétention de savoir mieux que lui ce qui vient de lui arriver.

« L'état cataleptique où je m'étais trouvé pendant plusieurs jours me fut expliqué scientifiquement, et les récits de ceux qui m'avaient vu ainsi me causaient une sorte d'irritation, quand je voyais qu'on attribuait à l'aberration d'esprit les mouvements ou les paroles coïncidant avec les diverses phases de *ce qui constituait pour moi une série d'événements logiques.* »

Celui qui parle ainsi se rit de la raison humaine qui le juge, et sa logique n'est pas la nôtre. Il semble s'adresser à nous du sein d'un état de connaissance où les notions de bon sens et de folie auraient cessé de former une insoluble contradiction. Rien n'est plus présomptueux, en face de si tranquilles affirmations, que l'hypothèse selon laquelle *Aurélia* serait le plaidoyer de Nerval, soucieux de sauver sa réputation et de démontrer qu'il était « guéri ». Je sais bien qu'il y a les lettres à son père : « Je n'ai point souffert, et je ne puis dire que ma raison ait été sérieusement attaquée (21 octobre 1853)... J'entreprends d'écrire et de constater toutes les impressions que m'a laissées ma maladie. Ce ne sera pas une étude inutile pour la médecine et pour la science. Jamais je ne me suis reconnu plus de facilité d'analyse et de description » (décembre 1854).

Je sais bien qu'écrivant au Dr Blanche, il le supplie d'excuser ses singularités auprès des dames de la clinique : « Expliquez-leur que l'être pensif qu'elles ont vu se traîner, inquiet et morose, dans le salon, au jardin, ou le long de votre table hospitalière, n'était pas moi-même assurément... Je renie le sycophante qui m'avait pris mon nom et peut-être mon visage » (31 mai 1854).

Je sais aussi qu'il a fait des efforts désespérés pour qu'on n'aille pas le croire sombré, et que la diminution de ses forces créatrices l'inquiétait autant que les difficultés matérielles à quoi l'exposait son incapacité de produire : « Je travaille et j'enfante dans la douleur », écrit-il à Antony Deschamps en octobre 1854 ; et à Georges Bell, dès l'hiver précédent : « Ce que j'écris en ce moment tourne trop dans un cercle restreint. Je me nourris de ma propre substance et ne me renouvelle pas ».

Mais c'est une des plus fâcheuses habitudes de la critique moderne, asservie à la psychologie, que d'ajouter foi aux aveux épistolaires davantage qu'aux œuvres, sous prétexte que la correspondance est de la réalité vécue et que l'œuvre est « seulement » imaginaire. Rien n'est plus contraire à la nature même de la création artistique que ce point de vue. Pourquoi veut-on que la vie, saisie à ces profondeurs les plus obscures où l'art a sa source, soit moins vraie qu'en ses aspects quotidiens ? On méconnaît ainsi cette différence des plans qui sépare à jamais les simples données vécues de l'expérience essentielle ; de celle-ci, les faits extérieurs ne sauraient être que les matériaux, librement employés à des fins nouvelles. Il est une région où, dépouillé de l'accident, l'individu redevient créature humaine et se retrouve, dans la situation la plus dénudée, en face de l'univers, de la mort et des origines ; c'est dans cette conscience-là que naissent le mythe et le poème, et tout ce qui se passe en dehors de cette sphère la plus profonde est impuissant à expliquer ces naissances.

On sait assez, d'ailleurs, tout ce qu'une lettre a de momentané, tout ce qui s'y glisse nécessairement d'intentions immédiates, d'influences vagues du destinataire, et d'ignorance de soi-même. Celles que Gérard écrit à son père, on a tort de les invoquer contre le témoignage d'*Aurélia*. Dictées par cette tendre affection filiale et cette modestie — que l'on ne retrouve que dans les derniers billets, si tragiquement courtois, de Hœlderlin à sa mère, — elles ne prouvent rien que le pieux désir de tranquilliser le vieillard (qui n'en demandait pas davantage). Et le besoin croissant de rejoindre tous les souvenirs de son enfance, d'être avec eux en harmonie, fait que Gérard témoigne une tendresse extrême à son père, d'abord, mais aussi à ses oncles et à ses cousins. Par surcroît, la crainte d'offenser qui que ce soit et le désir de réparer des torts souvent minimes sont l'un des soucis constants de ses dernières années ; mais, plutôt que d'y chercher une explication des intentions d'*Aurélia*, on y peut discerner l'effet de cette profonde transformation, de cette naissance à un altruisme charitable qui, au terme de l'odyssée tragique, bénéficient de la lumière nouvellement conquise. Finalement, c'est la poésie qui change la vie, et non pas l'inverse.

Aurélia raconte bien un progrès, mais ce n'est qu'apparemment celui d'un malade qui retrouverait son équilibre mental. Sous cette histoire de la précaire guérison de Gérard, une autre histoire se déroule, aux aspects multiples et infiniment plus dramatiques. Il faut se résigner, pour mieux la comprendre, à la tirer de cette pénombre douce où, avec une discrétion admirable, Nerval l'a présentée. Le seul document qu'il faille consulter, c'est le texte lui-même, qu'il convient d'examiner de très près, sans craindre l'abus des citations précises (1).

**

L'œuvre est construite à des profondeurs diverses, qui tiennent à l'état de conscience exceptionnel auquel Nerval était parvenu

---

(1) Je cite le texte d'*Aurélia* d'après l'excellente édition qu'en a donnée au *Divan* M. H. CLOUARD, en indiquant toujours (car la succession des étapes intérieures importe) la partie et le chapitre : I, 2 ; II, 3, etc. Les lettres et fragments sont tirés de la *Correspondance* publiée par M. J. MARSAN au *Mercure* ou de la précieuse biographie de M. A. MARIE.

lorsqu'il l'écrivit. Deux ou trois réalités s'y enchevêtrent, ou plutôt deux ou trois perceptions différentes de la même réalité. En racontant ses quelques mois de crise, séparés par dix ans de relative paix intérieure, Nerval bouleverse à tout instant la suite apparente des événements ; son récit inclut peu à peu, en les ordonnant selon une durée toute subjective, les moments devenus symboliques d'une vie entière, les progrès et les détours d'un chemin sinueux et secret. C'est son destin dont Nerval tente de retracer la courbe, tel qu'il l'a revécu à la faveur du rêve et de la folie ; et il faut entendre ici le mot destin dans son sens métaphysique le plus vaste : non seulement la suite des hasards terrestres, mais le destin éternel qui remonte aux origines de l'être et qui s'achève au delà des limites où s'enferme notre brève existence. « Nous ne vivons jamais qu'en avant ou en arrière. » Tout l'effort de Nerval est de démontrer, moins à autrui qu'à lui-même, que ses visions sont le couronnement de ses aspirations mystiques, la lumière suprême dont la clarté rejaillit sur tout le chemin parcouru.

Cependant, cette courbe n'est pas unique à ses yeux, et il en recommence sans cesse le tracé, comme s'il était naturel que des interprétations diverses pussent être simultanées sans qu'aucune fût mise en doute ; chacune d'elles, pourtant, il l'énonce avec cette assurance, ce ton de certitude tranquille qui accompagne de façon assez paradoxale son humilité. Les découvertes qui lui permettent une souveraine ironie envers les médecins et les psychologues, pourraient l'emplir d'un orgueil nietzschéen ; tout au contraire, il pousse la modestie jusqu'à accepter à la fois tous les aspects multiples de son aventure, sans jamais y intervenir pour un choix entre les affirmations qui s'imposent à lui. Sans doute est-ce là la preuve la plus sûre de sa sincérité, qui se refuse à dire davantage que ce qu'il sait ; mais c'est, mieux encore, le signe d'un stade de conscience où cette simultanéité des contraires ne provoque plus aucun étonnement.

Car il n'y a pas trace d'incohérence dans *Aurélia*. Cette superposition de récits apparemment divergents n'est pas le fait, — comme ceux qui y voient un document pathologique se hâtent trop de le dire, — d'une faiblesse des pouvoirs logiques, d'une impuissance à coordonner des éléments épars. Le premier privilège de ceux qui demandent à l'extase les suprêmes révélations, n'est-il pas de se montrer oublieux des exigences rationnelles ?

On a relevé, dans le récit des faits réels que rapporte *Aurélia*, des erreurs de chronologie et d'évidentes déformations. Nerval ne dit pas tout et impose à ce qu'il dit une inflexion qu'ignorent souvent ses lettres, plus proches de l'événement. Mais il faut reconnaître à celui qui considère sa vie comme un mythe la liberté d'en disposer à sa guise, — liberté qui n'est pas seulement celle du poète, mais celle d'un homme pour qui la valeur symbolique prise par les événements importe plus que leur enchaînement dans le temps. S'il les détache ainsi de leur cohérence extérieure, c'est qu'il a besoin de ce passé nouveau qu'il se construit. Il faut imaginer ce que c'est qu'un être qui entreprend une œuvre de cet ordre. Il y engage autre chose que son talent et son intelligence ; il y joue ce qu'on ne peut appeler autrement que son salut. Il témoigne, non pas que « telle chose advint », mais que de telle chose il est arrivé à faire une étape de son chemin spirituel. Le fait ne signifie plus en lui-même, mais par la place qu'il tient dans le poème de l'initiation.

« Il y a des années d'angoisses, de rêves, de projets, qui voudraient se presser dans une phrase, dans un mot », lit-on déjà dans une des « Lettres à Aurélia ». Tout ce passé tend à sortir de son agencement fortuit, pour fournir une réponse aux interrogations urgentes de celui qui cherche le sens de sa vie et le sens de la vie. Aussi chaque moment des années écoulées revêt-il une double et triple valeur symbolique ; Nerval raconte à la fois cette transformation du réel en symbole, le cours extérieur de sa maladie, la conquête du pardon accordé à ses fautes et enfin, tout au fond, le mythe de la rédemption universelle.

*
* *

La plus visible de ces courbes simultanées décrit la métamorphose d'une image féminine : l'actrice Jenny Colon, Aurélia, devient la Médiatrice, Isis, la Vierge. Mais cette histoire se moque du temps : l'évolution accomplie dans les dernières années transforme le passé tout entier, éclaire jusqu'aux plus lointains souvenirs. L'enfance elle-même de Gérard subit l'influence de cette métamorphose récente, car cette enfance aussi est arrachée à l'enchaînement des jours successifs, libérée de son insertion dans le devenir extérieur, pour n'être plus que l'objet d'une mémoire vivante et en quelque sorte intemporelle. Inscrite dans une autre succession, soumise à la seule loi de la conscience présente et de son anxieuse interrogation, l'époque où Nerval vivait à Mortefontaine entre dans le même mythe que les années de la maturité. Adrienne et Sophie Dawes, silhouettes féminines du plus lointain passé, quittent leur entourage enfantin pour devenir les

incarnations premières de Jenny : et c'est
l'histoire de *Sylvie*. On peut saisir le moment où cet épisode passe de sa signification immédiate à une nouvelle lumière.
Dans une lettre de 1852, Nerval raconte
une première fois l'histoire des costumes
anciens, trouvés dans un grenier et que
les deux jeunes gens revêtent. Ce n'est
encore qu'une évocation mélancolique et
charmante : « O tendre souvenir des aïeux !
brillants costumes, profanés dans une nuit
de folie, que vous m'avez coûté de larmes ! »
Sylvie, qui est de 1853, fait entrer le
regret de cet amour d'enfance dans le
cycle fatal de l'actrice aimée, perdue et
poursuivie. Les deux images, — celle,
déjà fabuleuse, d'Adrienne enfouie dans
un couvent et dont la mémoire a fait une
première forme de Jenny, celle de la
simple Sylvie toute terrestre et réelle, —
s'opposent, et le récit est tout tissu du
contraste entre ces deux amours, l'un et
l'autre insaisissables. Le sens en est pré-
cisé dans un délicieux fragment, supprimé
dans la version définitive.

« O nuit ! j'en ai peu connu de plus

belles : je ne sais pourquoi, dans les rêveries vagues qui m'étaient venues par moments, deux figures aimées se combattaient dans mon esprit : l'une semblait descendre des étoiles, et l'autre monter de la terre. La dernière disait : Je suis simple et fraîche comme les fleurs des champs ; l'autre : Je suis noble et pure comme les beautés immortelles conçues dans le sein de Dieu... »

Mais *Aurélia*, l'année suivante, considère comme sacrilège la confrontation des deux images. Évoquant Saint-Germain, où se passa la scène des costumes, Nerval un instant est tenté de suivre cette pente de la mémoire, mais il s'interrompt aussitôt.

« Il y avait là une terrasse ombragée de tilleuls qui rappelait aussi le souvenir de jeunes filles, de parentes, parmi lesquelles j'avais grandi. Une d'elles... Mais opposer ce vague amour d'enfance à celui qui a dévoré ma jeunesse, y avais-je songé seulement ? » (II, 2.)

Ainsi, le mythe a continué à transformer le passé : à Gérard il commande d'oublier tout ce qui n'est pas lui, pour ne point blasphémer Celle qui fut Adrienne, puis Jenny, et qui va devenir la Médiatrice. Ce même refus de s'attacher à la forme accidentelle des choses est nettement indiqué par un fragment des manuscrits d'*Aurélia*. Après avoir évoqué la bague, sciée par l'orfèvre, d'où il a cru voir couler du sang (I, 7), Gérard s'arrête : « Mais pourquoi dérouler ces souvenirs de billets jaunis et de fleurs fanées ? Mon cœur repose sous ces débris ; mais cette passion est l'histoire de toutes : *je ne veux qu'indiquer l'influence qu'elle a pu avoir sur les rêves de mon esprit* ».

Tout, ainsi, se recompose autour de l'événement central et profond (M. A. Marie et M. P. Audiat ont décelé bien d'autres métamorphoses subies par des faits réels). Le point de sa vie où Gérard a rencontré l'actrice devient, dans une connaissance semblable à celle du rêve et comme elle ignorante du temps, le point initial, antérieur à l'enfance elle-même. Nerval est parvenu à l'une de ces étapes spirituelles où l'on est le maître du passé aussi bien que du présent ou de l'avenir. Le renoncement, — forcé ou spontané, peu importe, — à l'amour de Jenny et à sa réalisation terrestre, déclenche en lui cette lente désadaptation qu'il appelle « l'épanchement du songe dans la vie réelle » (I, 3); dès lors, sa vie entière passe sur le plan du rêve, où l'esprit confère aux objets leur valeur multiple et changeante.

Toutes les précisions sur l'aventure réelle qu'il avait données encore dans *Sylvie*, il les écarte désormais. Déjà dans les *Petits châteaux de Bohême*, songeant à la dernière entrevue de Bruxelles à laquelle fera encore allusion la *Pandora*, il avait dit : « Une longue histoire, qui s'est dénouée dans un pays du Nord, — et qui ressemble à tant d'autres ! » Et à la seconde page d'*Aurélia*, il marquait le même dédain de ce qui fut : « Une dame que j'avais aimée longtemps et que j'appellerai du nom d'Aurélia, était perdue pour moi. *Peu importent les circonstances* de cet événement qui devait avoir une si grande influence sur ma vie... ». Seule lui importe maintenant l'expérience mystique qu'a inaugurée en lui l'échec de son amour. Et, vivante encore, Jenny commence ce voyage vers la figure mythique, qui est toute l'histoire de la folie de Nerval. Lors du dernier revoir « dans une froide capitale du Nord », l'accueil de l'actrice lui paraît déjà avoir « une valeur inexprimable, comme si *quelque chose de la religion* se mêlait aux douceurs d'un amour jusque-là profane, et lui imprimait le caractère de l'éternité » (I, 2). Bientôt, la mort de Jenny accomplira un pas décisif dans cette voie : « Elle m'appartenait bien plus dans sa mort que dans sa vie » (I, 7).

Mais ce n'est là que la première désincarnation. Morte même, Jenny reste une personne réelle, continue pour quelque temps à être l'actrice adorée. De longues années achèveront la métamorphose. Le besoin de croire qu'elle existe toujours commande toute la seconde partie d'*Aurélia ;* celle qu'il ne peut plus espérer revoir sur la terre, il faut qu'une croyance vienne le persuader qu'il la retrouvera ailleurs. La certitude, cependant, n'est pas conquise du premier coup. Avant de se fondre dans l'image d'Isis, Jenny encore tout humaine devient le modèle de piété auquel Gérard souhaite de pouvoir se conformer.

« Elle, pourtant, croyait à Dieu, et j'ai surpris un jour le nom de Jésus sur ses lèvres. Il en coulait si doucement que j'en ai pleuré. O mon Dieu, cette larme, — cette larme... Elle est séchée depuis si longtemps ! Cette larme, mon Dieu ! rendez-la-moi ! » (II, 1.)

Les visions, bientôt, interviennent, imposant l'image d'une Aurélia médiatrice, qui peut préparer à Gérard la voix du salut. Dans la première partie déjà, la faute commise qui hante son cerveau était apparue comme une faute envers la femme aimée, outrage dont il n'espérait pas le pardon (I, 1), ou abandon à de «faciles amours» (I, 9). Mais maintenant, le pardon attendu de l'actrice se confond peu à peu avec le pardon de Dieu lui-même pour une faute plus grave, qui fut de ne pas prêter une oreille assez attentive aux avertissements de la première crise. Dans un instant du plus sombre désespoir, Gérard s'écriera : « Je comprends, — elle a fait un dernier effort pour me sauver ; — j'ai manqué le moment suprême où le pardon était possible encore. Du haut du ciel, elle pouvait prier pour moi l'Époux divin... » (II, 3).

Puis, sur le double plan du rêve et du réel, la confusion entre Jenny et l'ange intercesseur s'accentue. Lorsque, dans sa détresse, Gérard tombe à genoux devant une image de la Vierge, il se souvient soudain qu'Aurélia lui a échappé, et son cri d'angoisse : « La Vierge est morte et tes prières sont inutiles » (II, 4) témoigne bien à quel point l'identification s'est faite déjà. L'étape dernière est proche, et ce sont les paroles solennelles de la vision merveilleuse :

« Je suis la même que Marie, la même que ta mère, la même aussi que sous toutes les formes tu as toujours aimée. A chacune de tes épreuves, j'ai quitté l'un des masques dont je voile mes traits, et bientôt tu me verras telle que je suis... » (II,5.)

Il vaut la peine de remarquer qu'à l'instant où Aurélia se confond avec la Mère céleste, elle rejoint aussi l'image de

la mère de Gérard, qu'il avait à peine
connue : elle était morte alors qu'il avait
deux ans, pendant les campagnes napo-
léoniennes où elle avait suivi son mari ;
mais cette image n'en était pas moins restée,
pour Nerval, l'un des symboles de sa religion. Dans un rêve destiné à figurer dans
Aurélia, une femme vêtue de noir, aux
larmes de diamant, lui semble être le
spectre de sa mère. Et deux lettres, des
25 et 27 novembre 1853 (M. A. Marie
donne le 29 novembre 1810 pour la date
de la mort de Mme Labrunie) montrent
bien quelles mystérieuses attaches le
liaient à ce souvenir. Au Dr Blanche, il
écrit : « Or c'est assez faire le fou quand
on est raisonnable, et ce n'est pas le jour
anniversaire de la mort de ma mère que
j'en aurai le courage ». Et à l'un de ses
cousins : « Aujourd'hui, jour anniversaire
de celui où ma pauvre mère est morte en
Silésie, suivant le drapeau de la France,
mais laissant son fils orphelin, je me suis
promis de vivre enfin sérieusement ». Mais,
dès l'instant où toutes les figures tutélaires
se sont réunies en une seule, dans les grandes

visions lumineuses de la Réconciliation
finale, l'image de Jenny-Aurélia ne reprendra plus les traits de la femme réelle,
enveloppe momentanée parmi d'autres, qui
n'étaient que les ébauches annonciatrices
de Celle qui pardonne.

La lente transformation qui fait passer
un être de la vie réelle à un état angélique
rapproche cette expérience de Nerval
d'autres illuminations romantiques. C'est
ainsi que la mort de sa fiancée inaugura
pour Novalis la transfiguration de la vie
entière que racontent les pages de son
Journal et qui aboutit aux *Hymnes à la
Nuit*. Hœlderlin, séparé de Diotima puis
apprenant sa mort, commença à se déséprendre de lui-même et à entrer dans le
personnage sous lequel, durant de longues
années, il s'isola du monde des hommes.
Et Hoffmann, faisant de Julia Marc une
créature unique et mystérieuse, attend la
mort qui lui permettra de « contempler
dans l'existence véritable celle qui fut son
désir, son espoir et sa consolation en un
temps de ténèbres infernales. » Plus que
tout autre, enfin, Maurice de Guérin,

méditant sur la mort de Marie, répondra à la douleur par un héroïsme qui rappelle celui de Nerval ; bien que le sentiment qu'il vouait à la morte ne fût pas tout à fait un amour, il atteindra à une extase où lui sera faite la promesse de retrouver un jour l'amie perdue.

*
* *

Mais toute tragédie est unique, et ces analogies ne doivent pas nous arrêter. Il reste, dans *Aurélia*, tout un élément proprement nervalien, un itinéraire particulier, qui n'est ni la magie de Novalis, ni la comédie solennelle de Hœlderlin, qui ne peut pas davantage aboutir, comme chez Hoffmann, au sacrifice de l'artiste, qu'à l'extase panthéiste comme chez Guérin. Si Nerval a poursuivi le souvenir d'une amie perdue, jusqu'aux royaumes inconnus où les âmes se changent en quelque essence divine, il a donné à cette poursuite un sens qu'elle n'a eu que pour lui. En même temps qu'il raconte la tranfiguration de Jenny, il s'attache à une autre pensée, dont celle-là n'est qu'un symbole plus transparent. Il nous faut suivre maintenant sa destinée selon une courbe plus intérieure encore, qui est, comme la première, l'histoire d'un triomphe laborieusement obtenu à travers les souffrances. Les visions dont *Aurélia* fixe le souvenir, sombres d'abord, finissent par se faire lumineuses à mesure que l'identification de Jenny avec l'Ange se précise. Mais Nerval raconte cette naissance de la lumière en lui donnant encore une signification plus urgente.

Selon cette courbe nouvelle, *Aurélia*, en même temps que la formation d'une figure mythique, décrit une série d'épreuves imposées à Gérard pour racheter une faute commise. Voie du salut personnel, qui s'achève par l'aurore de la Rédemption. L'une de ces évolutions s'appuie sur l'autre, et notre logique seule dissocie ces deux valeurs du symbole, entre lesquelles Nerval lui-même a vu un lien étroit :

« Je veux expliquer comment, éloigné longtemps de la vraie route, je m'y suis senti ramené par le souvenir chéri d'une personne morte, et comment le besoin de croire qu'elle existait toujours a fait rentrer dans mon esprit le sentiment précis des diverses vérités que je n'avais pas assez fermement recueillies en mon âme. » (II, 4.)

Cette phrase est l'une de celles où se résume avec le plus d'assurance le chemin parcouru. Elle est l'une des clefs que Nerval donne de son œuvre. Ce n'est plus seulement le passage d'un état de conscience « normal » à un autre, que l'on peut appeler « mythique », mais un progrès intérieur, la conquête de certaines croyances. De cette conquête, on peut décrire les étapes.

Dans la première partie du récit, qui sur le plan des faits raconte la crise de 1841, Gérard subit, sans encore l'interpréter, sans se poser en face d'elle, l'invasion du rêve. Le thème de la faute n'y apparaît qu'en sourdine, sous la forme d'un outrage envers Jenny. Pourtant, après la dernière vision, la plus dramatique de toutes, la culpabilité prend soudain le sens d'un blasphème, d'un péché de la créature contre Dieu. Nerval se demande s'il n'a pas cédé à la démesure en voulant faire de son existence terrestre une lutte contre son double, contre la folie, qui peut-être, — il croit le comprendre soudain, — lui avait été accordée par quelque dieu bienveillant. Au cri de la révolte :

« Eh bien luttons contre l'esprit fatal, luttons contre le dieu lui-même avec les armes de la tradition et de la science. Quoi qu'il fasse dans l'ombre et la nuit, j'existe, — et j'ai pour le vaincre tout le temps qu'il m'est donné encore de vivre sur la terre » (I, 9)
répond maintenant le doute de celui qui se croit damné :

« J'étais maudit peut-être pour avoir voulu percer un mystère redoutable en offensant la loi divine ; je ne devais plus attendre que la colère et le mépris ! Les ombres irritées fuyaient en jetant des cris et traçant dans l'air des cercles fatals, comme les oiseaux à l'approche d'un orage. » (I, 10.)

C'est sur cette splendide image d'effroi tragique que s'achève la première partie d'*Aurélia*. Mais ce n'est pas encore la forme dernière du sentiment de la faute. Bien loin d'avoir péché en voulant percer le mystère de ce qui lui arrivait, n'a-t-il pas eu tort de sortir de sa première démence sans deviner qu'elle lui faisait un devoir de changer d'existence ? Cette inquiétude lui vient après une vision qui suit une visite à la tombe d'Aurélia.

« Dieu m'avait laissé ce temps pour me repentir, et je n'en avais point profité. — Après la visite du *convive de pierre*, je m'étais rassis au festin. » (II, 3.)

Touchant alors le fond du désespoir, il voit lui apparaître une première lueur. La folie ne pourrait-elle être un avertissement d'en haut ? ou bien, puisque cette infortune lui est envoyée, ne peut-il lui-même, par un effort conscient, s'emparer d'elle et la transformer en une série d'épreuves ? Le terme de ce calvaire, s'il a la force d'y parvenir, serait le pardon de la faute mystérieuse qui pèse sur lui, sans qu'il en sache la vraie nature. D'Allemagne, en juillet 1854, il écrit au Dr Blanche : « Je me fie en cette pensée que je n'ai jamais voulu mal faire... Si j'étais destiné à donner l'exemple de la plus douloureuse *expiation* qu'on peut imaginer, je m'y soumettrais *volontiers* ».

Et dans ses papiers, on a retrouvé cette note, où se révèle mieux encore le sens qu'il commence à donner à son état :

« Il est encore temps. L'Écriture dit qu'un repentir suffit pour être sauvé... Et si l'événement qui vous frappe empêche ce repentir ? *Et si l'on vous met en état de fièvre, de folie ? Si l'on vous bouche les portes de la rédemption ?* »

C'est là le cri de révolte le plus terrible qu'il ait jamais articulé. En un moment où la détresse le plonge dans la nuit la plus obscure, il éprouve toute l'injustice de son sort. La folie, qui s'est abattue sur lui, le tient prisonnier, l'empêche de s'engager dans la voie du rachat. Va-t-il succomber ? Quel recours lui reste-t-il ? A quoi sert donc toute sa bonne volonté, si « on » s'obstine à ne pas lui tendre la main ?

L'héroïsme de Nerval prend sa grandeur pleine au fond même de cet abîme où il se débat. Il ne poussera qu'une fois le cri de protestation. Puis il se met à scruter sa mémoire, à fouiller tout le passé des rêves et des aventures réelles, à écrire *Aurélia :* ah ! certes pas pour expliquer

aux psychologues ce qui lui est arrivé !
Il a une besogne bien plus pressée à accomplir : il faut surmonter le malheur, trouver
la formule magique qui métamorphosera
cette chaîne d'infortunes en une échelle
de salut. Ce n'est pas seulement de raconter qu'il s'agit maintenant, — et ce qu'il
y avait encore de jeu nostalgique dans les
évocations de *Sylvie* ne reparaîtra plus
dans l'œuvre nouvelle, — mais d'avoir
raison du malheur inexplicable et injuste,
d'en faire, par une prise de conscience et
par un acte de volonté, une expiation qui
aura sa récompense. A tout instant, cette
intention héroïque transparaît, et le mot
d'« épreuves » revient, comme la bouée
à laquelle il s'accroche. Dans la vision
merveilleuse, celle qui est la même que
Marie, la même que sa mère, lui parle de
ses épreuves (II, 5). Et c'est dans cette pensée
qu'il trouve la force de résister, lorsque,
transporté à Passy chez le Dr Blanche, il
est tenté de se laisser aller à la folie qui
le menace.

« Je compris, en me voyant parmi les
aliénés, que tout n'avait été pour moi

qu'illusions jusque-là. *Toutefois*, les promesses que j'attribuais à la déesse Isis me semblaient se réaliser par une série d'épreuves que j'étais destiné à subir. Je les acceptai donc avec résignation. » (II, 5).

Par instants, il cherche dans les croyances occultes ou orientales qu'il avait souvent caressées les formules qui exprimeraient cette ascension vers le salut. Il salue le lever du soleil par des prières, se croit initié à quelque rite mystérieux destiné à rétablir le monde dans son harmonie primitive. Tout lui devient signe, symbole, complicité mystique. Comme dans les *Vers Dorés* de 1845 :

> *Respecte dans la bête un esprit agissant :*
> *Chaque fleur est une âme à la Nature éclose ;*
> *Un mystère d'amour dans le métal repose ;*
> *« Tout est sensible ! » Et tout sur ton être est puissant.*
>
> . . . .
> *Souvent dans l'être obscur habite un Dieu caché ;*
> *Et comme un œil naissant couvert par ses paupières,*
> *Un pur esprit s'accroît sous l'écorce des pierres !*

il sacrifie à un « pythagorisme » qui, — non sans rappeler les convictions auxquelles

Hugo parvenait à la même date, — lui inspire cette page parfaite :

« Du moment que je me fus assuré que j'étais soumis aux épreuves de l'initiation sacrée, une force invincible entra dans mon esprit. Je me jugeais un héros vivant sous le regard des dieux ; tout dans la nature prenait des aspects nouveaux, et des voix secrètes sortaient de la plante, de l'arbre, des animaux, des plus humbles insectes, pour m'avertir et m'encourager. Le langage de mes compagnons avait des tours mystérieux dont je comprenais le sens, les objets sans forme et sans vie se prêtaient eux-mêmes aux calculs de mon esprit ; — des combinaisons de cailloux, des figures d'angles, de fentes ou d'ouvertures, des découpures de feuilles, des couleurs, des odeurs et des sons, je voyais ressortir des harmonies jusqu'alors inconnues. — Comment, me disais-je, ai-je pu exister si longtemps hors de la nature et sans m'identifier à elle ? Tout vit, tout agit, tout se correspond ; les rayons magnétiques émanés de moi-même ou des autres traversent sans obstacle la chaîne infinie des choses créées ; c'est un réseau transparent qui couvre le monde, et dont les fils déliés se communiquent de proche en proche aux planètes et aux étoiles. Captif en ce moment sur la terre, je m'entretiens avec le chœur des astres, qui prend part à mes joies et à mes douleurs ! » (II, 6.)

Ces phrases légères, où l'on pourrait trouver toute une esthétique baudelairienne et qui ne sont pas sans jeter une vive lumière sur le mystère poétique des *Chimères*, sont pleines de réminiscences occultistes ; mais précisément, on sent ici, par la vertu même d'un style qui ne saurait tromper, combien le goût de Nerval pour les lectures mystiques était autre chose qu'un divertissement littéraire : une sympathie profonde, qui lui fait ici trouver, en plein drame métaphysique, une singulière euphorie dans cette contemplation d'un univers où tout est correspondance et parole.

Mais ce n'est pas là encore le terme de ses interrogations. Ces mêmes théories l'amènent à « se demander compte de sa vie, et même de ses existences antérieures ». Il cherche à se tranquilliser en se disant que son existence actuelle pourrait être « une suffisante expiation ». « Cette pensée me rassura, mais ne m'ôta pas la crainte d'être à jamais classé parmi les malheureux. » (II, 6.) Il faudra toute une série de visions encore pour que son ciel s'éclaircisse et que se réalise l'espoir qu'il a mis dans sa soumission aux épreuves. Enfin, Aurélia lui apparaît dans le premier « rêve délicieux » pour lui annoncer la délivrance : « L'épreuve à laquelle tu étais soumis est venue à son terme ; ces escaliers sans nombre que tu te fatiguais à descendre ou à gravir, étaient les liens mêmes des anciennes illusions qui embarrassaient ta pensée... » (II, 6). Dans les visions suivantes, elle revient sans cesse sous des apparences magnifiques, ses grands yeux dévorant l'espace, sa longue chevelure imprégnée des parfums de l'Yémen volant dans l'air, transfigurée et radieuse aux côtés du Messie. « Courage, frère, c'est la dernière étape » et le ciel du pardon s'ouvre dans toute sa gloire (II, 7).

Le pardon final a été acquis par l'action héroïque et, en même temps, par un altruisme qui a mérité la récompense. Ce thème de l'acte charitable est tout entremêlé à celui de la conquête du salut par les épreuves acceptées. La première partie d'*Aurélia* ne le fait pas encore intervenir, mais dès la seconde, le besoin d'être bon envers autrui se fait sentir. C'est d'abord la visite à un ami malade. « Quand on se sent malheureux, on songe au malheur des autres. » (I, 1.) C'est ensuite le convoi funèbre d'un inconnu, que Gérard suit jusqu'au cimetière, trouvant quelque consolation à penser que ce mort serait content de se voir accompagné par un frère de douleur. « Cette idée me fit verser des larmes... O larmes bénies, depuis longtemps votre douceur m'était refusée ! Ma tête se dégageait, et un rayon d'espoir me guidait encore. » (II, 2.) Puis c'est l'aumône donnée à une chanteuse dans un café, et de nouveau le même sentiment heureux (II, 4). Peu après, dans une crise où il se prend de querelle avec un facteur, voyant soudain celui-ci fondre en larmes, Gérard s'attendrit lui-même et s'en va prier à Saint-Eustache. Comme il en sort, et se promène au Jardin des Plantes, la pluie se met à tomber et il s'apitoie sur les femmes et les enfants qui vont être mouillés (II, 5).

Il est remarquable que tous ces mouvements de charité soient postérieurs à la résolution de prêter l'oreille aux avertissements d'en haut. Mais on peut admettre aussi que Gérard fut mis sur cette voie par les efforts du Dr Blanche, dont on ne fera jamais assez l'éloge. Quoiqu'un incendie ait détruit toutes les notes qu'il avait prises sur la maladie de Nerval et qu'on ne puisse guère suivre son traitement qu'à travers les allusions de celui-ci et les lettres qu'il lui écrivait, on devine l'intelligente discrétion de son assistance. Dans une lettre à Antony Deschamps, écrite en octobre 1854, à l'instant où il avait obtenu par mille ruses de sortir de la clinique, Gérard confesse la reconnaissance qu'il garde à son médecin : « J'ai trop souffert de quelques remèdes auxquels je n'ai pu me soustraire pour ne pas approuver le système de notre ami Émile, qui n'a employé que les bains et deux ou trois purgations contre le mal dont j'ai été frappé, mais qui m'a traité moralement et guéri, je le reconnais, de bien des défauts que je me reconnaissais sans oser les avouer ». Le récit d'*Aurélia* permet d'entrevoir mieux ce que fut ce traitement moral. Au lieu de juger son malade selon des catégories médicales préconçues, le Dr Blanche entra autant qu'il était possible dans son univers et chercha à provoquer là les rencontres favorables. C'est ainsi qu'il le fit assister au pénible traitement auquel il fallait soumettre un jeune aliéné : comme il s'obstinait à refuser toute nourriture, on devait le sustenter de force, à l'aide d'un tuyau de caoutchouc introduit par le nez. Le récit de Gérard montre combien le Dr Blanche a vu juste en lui proposant ce spectacle.

« Abandonné jusque-là au cercle monotone de mes sensations ou de mes souffrances morales, je rencontrais un être indéfinissable, taciturne et patient, assis comme un sphinx aux portes suprêmes de l'existence. Je me pris à l'aimer à cause de son malheur et de son abandon, et *je me sentis relevé par cette sympathie et par cette pitié.* Il me semblait, placé ainsi entre la mort et la vie, comme un interprète sublime, comme un confesseur prédestiné à entendre ces secrets de l'âme que la parole n'oserait transmettre ou ne réussirait pas à rendre. C'était l'oreille de Dieu sans le mélange de la pensée d'un autre. Je passais des heures entières à m'examiner mentalement, la tête penchée sur la sienne et lui tenant les mains. Il me semblait qu'un certain magnétisme réunissait nos deux esprits, et je me sentis ravi quand la première fois une parole sortit de sa bouche. On n'en voulait rien croire, et j'attribuais à mon ardente volonté ce commencement de guérison. Cette nuit-là, *j'eus un rêve délicieux, le premier depuis bien longtemps.* » (II,6). Reconnaissant envers celui qu'il considérait comme son sauveur, Gérard raconte qu'il passa des heures encore à lui chanter des chansons populaires.

Ainsi, la lumière qui éclate à la fin d'*Aurélia* a été retrouvée par les deux voies de l'expiation et de la charité. Est-ce à dire que, triomphant de la tentation « orientale », Nerval avait trouvé le salut dans un retour aux croyances chrétiennes ? La Vierge succédant à Isis, l'apparition du Messie dans la vision splendide de la fin autoriseraient à le croire. Mais nous touchons ici à une nouvelle question, à une autre des courbes de ce destin aux inépuisables profondeurs.

*
* *

Car, si évident soit-il pour Nerval lui-même que le rêve et la veille se soient conjugués pour former la voie du rachat, que la pitié ait opéré une irruption de lumière, ce n'est encore là qu'un second plan de réalité, qui trouve sa solution dans cette vie, dans « une force nouvelle à opposer aux malheurs futurs ». Au delà de ce problème personnel mené ainsi jusqu'à l'apaisement, Nerval a aperçu des profondeurs et des voies ouvertes.

L'une sur le mythe cosmique et universel, où son destin particulier, dont les faits réels n'étaient que le symbole, devient à son tour l'image du destin de l'humanité.

L'autre voie précise les présents du rêve ; la conquête n'y est pas, cette fois-ci, de l'ordre du salut personnel ou collectif, mais de l'ordre de la connaissance : à son point extrême, le subjectivisme équivaut à la découverte d'une réalité nouvelle et rejoint une objectivité supérieure. « Le chemin mystérieux va vers l'intérieur », disait Novalis.

Ce n'est donc pas son propre salut seulement que Gérard, ajoutant à la guérison où le guidait le Dr Blanche la sagesse inspirée par ses visions, a engagé et gagné. D'un bout à l'autre de l'œuvre, un autre pari, bien plus grave encore, se débat, sous la forme d'un vaste mythe du destin humain. Et *Aurélia*, qui paraissait n'être que la lutte d'un seul, le drame unique d'un cas original, s'élève à la grandeur d'une épopée métaphysique.

Cette nouvelle courbe, perceptible à travers toute la confession, s'amorce avec le thème de la mort, au cours d'une hallucination où Gérard entre en conversation avec son oncle, pour apparaître en pleine lumière dans les visions de la seconde partie : une fois les certitudes conquises, le héros descend « parmi les hommes pour leur annoncer la bonne nouvelle » (II, 7).

A la crainte du néant qu'exprime Gérard, l'oncle répond que matière et esprit sont immortels. « Notre passé et notre avenir sont solidaires. Nous vivons dans notre race, et notre race vit en nous ». Et aussitôt défile l'immense cortège de l'humanité ; mais la certitude s'évanouit dans une spéculation sur les nombres, la vision s'obscurcit, Gérard croit comprendre que « ces questions sont obscures ou dangereuses » (I, 5).

Le sentiment du défendu, du péril que comportent certaines questions plus qu'humaines, subsiste dans la suite de la vision où, descendu dans la cité des races successives, Nerval est arrêté par un homme vêtu de blanc, dont il distingue mal la figure et qui le menace d'un glaive, comme pour « l'empêcher de pénétrer le mystère de ces retraites ». Le monde d'innocence où il se trouve cherche en vain à le retenir : il est interdit à l'homme d'y séjourner. « Je me mis à pleurer à chaudes

larmes, comme au souvenir d'un paradis
perdu. Là, je sentis amèrement que j'étais
un passant dans ce monde à la fois étranger
et chéri, et je frémis à la pensée que je
devais retourner dans la vie. »

Ce sentiment du paradis perdu, d'un
pays de blancheur où nous échapperons
un jour à toutes les affres terrestres, c'est
la première forme, encore incertaine, fra-
gile, menacée, du mythe de l'immortalité
où Gérard trouvera la consolation finale.
Pour un instant, il vit une première fois
dans cette bienfaisante conviction. « Ainsi,
ce doute éternel de l'immortalité de l'âme
qui affecte les meilleurs esprits se trouvait
résolu pour moi. Plus de mort, plus de
tristesse, plus d'inquiétude », s'écrie-t-il
au sortir de cette « patrie mystique ».

Pourtant, le jour où, poursuivant une
étoile vers l'Orient, il errait dans les rues,
il avait refusé l'immortalité chrétienne :
« Non ! je n'appartiens pas à ton ciel. Dans
cette étoile sont ceux qui m'attendent. Ils
sont antérieurs à la révélation que tu as
annoncée. Laisse-moi les rejoindre… » (I, 2).
Et bien des fois encore, il se plaira à ces

imaginations qui lui représentent dans un astre ou dans la lune la vie délicieuse des âmes désincarnées.

Après la vision de la patrie mystique, un rêve vient confirmer cette pensée de l'immortalité assurée. Il se voit dans une salle, connue dans son enfance, où trois femmes portent en elles les traits de toutes ses parentes à la fois ; lui-même est vêtu d'un petit habit brun, tissé de fils ténus comme ceux de l'araignée, « coquet, gracieux et imprégné de douces odeurs ». Mais ce rêve, où s'exprime si bien la nostalgie de l'innocence enfantine, s'achève brusquement dans une tonalité lugubre. L'admirable jardin où il a suivi l'une des femmes se change en un cimetière, sa compagne disparaît, et au long d'un mur, il aperçoit un buste renversé, dont le visage a les traits d'Aurélia, cependant que des voix clament : « L'univers est dans la nuit ! » (I, 6). Dans ces images funèbres, il voit le signe certain de la mort d'Aurélia, mais il se persuade encore qu'il la reverra dans le monde entrevu (I, 7).

La préoccupation subsiste, pourtant, et

se manifeste par la volonté d'écrire une histoire de la création, dont une nouvelle vision lui montre l'étrange paysage primitif, chaos monstrueux, où croissent cependant les germes de la clarté. Toute une cosmogonie, inspirée de traditions orientales, se déroule dans une extraordinaire splendeur d'évocation : métamorphoses et combats des monstres, naissance des humains, évolution des races à travers les luttes et les réconciliations.

« Tout à coup une singulière harmonie résonna dans nos solitudes, et il semblait que les cris, les rugissements, et les sifflements confus des êtres primitifs se modulassent désormais sur cet air divin. Les variations se succédaient à l'infini, la planète s'éclairait peu à peu, des formes divines se dessinaient sur la verdure et sur la profondeur des bocages, et, désormais domptés, tous les monstres que j'avais vus dépouillaient leurs formes bizarres et devenaient hommes et femmes... » (I,8).

Le même accord de la musique et des formes se poursuit dans les pages suivantes, où se tait et s'élève sans cesse « l'hymne interrompu de la terre et des cieux ». Mais la vision se brouille sur des scènes tragiques.

« Je vois encore, sur un pic baigné des eaux, une femme abandonnée, qui crie, les cheveux épars, se débattant contre la mort. Ses accents plaintifs dominaient le bruit des eaux... Fut-elle sauvée ? Je l'ignore. Les dieux, ses frères, l'avaient condamnée ; mais au-dessus de sa tête brillait l'Étoile du soir qui versait sur son front des rayons enflammés. »

Puis la signification de cette image s'enrichit de souvenirs mythiques : « Partout mourait, pleurait, languissait, l'image souffrante de la Mère éternelle. »

Pour longtemps, les rêves de Gérard restent terrifiants ; l'apparition du Double, déjà entrevue dans une hallucination éveillée, met le comble à l'épouvante. Une idée affreuse s'impose : « L'homme est double, me dis-je... Il y a en tout homme un spectateur et un acteur, celui qui parle et celui qui répond. Les Orientaux ont vu là deux ennemis : le bon et le mauvais génie. — Suis-je le bon, suis-je le mauvais ?

me disais-je. En tout cas, *l'autre* m'est hostile... Qui sait s'il n'y a pas telle circonstance ou tel âge où ces deux esprits se séparent ? Attachés au même corps tous deux par une affinité matérielle, peut-être l'un est-il promis à la gloire et au bonheur, l'autre à l'anéantissement, ou à la souffrance éternelle ? » (I, 9).

Jamais son être n'a été si près de se défaire et de lui échapper. Double lui-même, il croit apercevoir doubles tous ceux qui l'entourent. Le souvenir manifeste d'une scène lue jadis dans les *Élixirs du Diable* de son cher Hoffmann lui inspire la crainte que « l'autre », profitant de l'erreur universelle, n'aille consommer le mariage mystique qui se prépare entre Aurélia et lui. C'est à cet instant, dans cette angoisse la pire de toutes, qu'il a un sursaut de révolte et décide de lutter contre le dieu. En ce moment essentiel, le même tournant décisif change, sur tous les plans où il se déroule à la fois, l'orientation du poème d'*Aurélia*. Résolu à « employer toutes les forces de sa volonté », le malheureux se refuse à céder. Mais une

nouvelle vision l'abat, le rejette hors de
« l'univers magique » où était possible
l'immortalité de l'âme ; et le sentiment
de la malédiction clôt la première partie
du livre.

Dans la seconde, le mouvement va, sur le
plan métaphysique comme sur les autres,
du pire abîme de ténèbres à l'éclosion de
la lumière. Dès les premières lignes, le
thème de la mort revient, non pas sous
forme d'un rêve cette fois, mais comme
une interrogation précise, à laquelle il
faudra donner une réponse si le drame
personnel doit avoir une fin. L'un et l'autre
s'enchevêtrent désormais plus étroitement
encore : les étapes de la lutte sont projetées
du plan individuel sur celui du mythe
cosmique, et en retour il faudra que la
lumière pénètre celui-ci, pour que sur
l'autre Gérard trouve la paix finale. Dans
la première crise, il était resté passif
encore, subissant l'invasion des angoisses
et des menaces ; dans la seconde, il prend
une conscience de plus en plus nette de
la nécessité qui lui impose de satisfaire
aux grandes questions métaphysiques, sur-

gies dans son esprit sous l'imminence du naufrage. Il sait désormais qu'il n'y aura de solution à son problème que s'il trouve celle du problème humain. Le passage est très visible dans ces lignes qui ouvrent la seconde partie, placée sous le signe d'Eurydice :

« Une seconde fois perdue !

« Tout est fini, tout est passé ! C'est moi maintenant qui dois mourir, et mourir sans espoir ! — *Qu'est-ce donc que la mort ?* Si c'était le néant... Plût à Dieu ! Mais Dieu lui-même ne peut faire que la mort soit le néant.

« Pourquoi donc est-ce la première fois, depuis si longtemps, que je songe à *lui* ? Le système fatal qui s'était créé dans mon esprit n'admettait pas cette royauté solitaire... ou plutôt elle s'absorbait dans la somme des êtres : c'était le dieu de Lucretius, impuissant et perdu dans son immensité. »

Ainsi, son erreur aurait été de s'attacher à ces visions cosmiques qu'il tenait de l'occultisme. Du fond de l'enfance, l'image de Jésus réapparaît, et ce souvenir s'associe à la piété d'Aurélia. Nerval fait alors entendre la plainte de sa génération, désireuse de religion, mais élevée en des jours d'orage, accoutumée trop tôt à une foi vague « dont l'adhésion indifférente est plus coupable peut-être que l'impiété et l'hérésie ». Comme il souhaiterait de pouvoir recourir, contre tout ce qui le menace, à une foi plus naïve ! « Lorsque l'âme flotte incertaine entre la vie et le rêve, entre le désordre de l'esprit et le retour à la froide réflexion, c'est dans la pensée religieuse que l'on doit chercher des secours. » Mais hélas, « il est bien difficile de reconstruire l'édifice mystique dont les innocents et les simples admettent dans leur cœur la figure toute tracée... L'ignorance ne s'apprend pas ». Reniant l'héritage critique du XVIIIe siècle, il s'écrie : « L'arbre de science n'est pas l'arbre de vie ! »

Son drame est à cet instant tout semblable à celui qui fait le sujet de la *Confession d'un enfant du siècle* et du *Prologue de Rolla :* « Je suis venu trop tard dans un monde trop vieux... Pauvre fils de Dieu qu'on oublie, on ne m'a pas appris à t'aimer...

> *« Pourquoi m'obsèdes-tu de cette soif ardente,*
> *Si tu ne connais pas de source où l'étancher ?*

Mais Musset resta le prisonnier de son incertitude, du doute et du blasphème. « Malgré lui l'infini le tourmente », mais pas un instant il n'est capable de cet effort de tout l'être qui se décide pour cela qui veut lui échapper et contre quoi sa raison s'insurge. Le même combat irrésolu entre un cœur qui voudrait croire et une intelligence qui s'en défend tint longtemps Hugo prisonnier avant les révélations de l'exil :

> *On dirait que j'attends quelqu'un qui n'ouvre pas !*
> *C'est notre mal, à nous enfants des passions.*
> . . . .
> *De quel nom te nommer, heure trouble où nous sommes?*
> *...Croyances, passions, désespoirs, espérances,*
> *Rien n'est dans le grand jour, et rien n'est dans la nuit.*
> . . . .
> *Une chose, ô Jésus, en secret m'épouvante,*
> *C'est l'écho de ta voix qui va s'affaiblissant.*

Nerval, comme ses contemporains, souffre de ce divorce entre le sentiment et la raison. Un instant, il est tenté par une réconciliation de la science et de la foi : « J'ai meilleur espoir de la bonté de Dieu : peut-être touchons-nous à l'époque prédite où la science, ayant accompli son cercle entier de synthèse et d'analyse, de croyance et de négation, pourra s'épurer elle-même et faire jaillir du désordre et des ruines la cité merveilleuse de l'avenir... Il ne faut pas faire si bon marché de la raison humaine, que de croire qu'elle gagne quelque chose à s'humilier tout entière, car ce serait accuser sa céleste origine... L'apôtre qui voulait toucher pour croire n'a pas été maudit pour cela ! »

Il n'en reste pas longtemps à ces espoirs de progrès, qui gardent peut-être quelque reflet de ses entretiens avec les ingénieurs saint-simoniens dont il avait été l'ami en Égypte. Mais il est singulier de voir cet homme, isolé par son drame, porter ainsi en lui toutes es tendances contradictoires de son époque, faire de son débat intérieur le champ clos où s'affrontent toutes les hypothèses d'un temps qui n'en fut pas avare. Il s'interrompt cependant : « Qu'ai-je écrit là ? Ce sont des blasphèmes. L'humilité chrétienne ne peut parler ainsi. De telles pensées sont loin d'attendrir l'âme. Elles ont sur le front les éclairs d'orgueil de la couronne de Satan... Un pacte avec Dieu lui-même ?... O science ! ô vanité ! » Pour défendre son esprit de ces idées, il se plonge dans l'étude de la cabale, revient à son cher « syncrétisme » qui reconnaissait à chaque religion une portion des arcanes divins, cherche à retrouver l'alphabet magique à travers ses formes diverses et brouillées, et s'arrête à une conception « analogique » de la création : « Le soleil, pareil à la plante qui le représente, qui de sa tête inclinée suit la révolution de sa marche céleste, semait sur la terre les germes féconds des plantes et des animaux... L'Esprit de l'Être-Dieu, reproduit et pour ainsi dire reflété sur la terre, devenait le type commun des âmes humaines, dont chacune, par suite, était à la fois homme et dieu ». Mais, il est pris aussitôt d'un scrupule : « J'ignore même si le sentiment qui en résulte n'est pas conforme à l'idée chrétienne ».

Une fois de plus, la crainte d'être maudit pour ses erreurs, d'avoir méconnu les avertissements divins, le tourmente. L'anxiété, cependant, se précise en un choix nécessaire : entre les croyances qu'il était allé chercher jadis en Orient et les promesses chrétiennes, il est impossible de tergiverser encore. Il lui faut renier toutes les formes de magie, tout cet attachement aux signes et aux idoles, auquel il a tant sacrifié. « Je comprends, se dit-il, j'ai préféré la créature au créateur ; j'ai déifié mon amour et j'ai adoré, selon les rites païens, celle dont le dernier soupir a été consacré au Christ. Mais si cette religion dit vrai, Dieu peut me pardonner encore » (II, 2). Quelque chose fait obstacle encore à toute conversion ; à son désir de confession s'opposent toujours la crainte d'une « religion redoutable » et les « préjugés philosophiques issus de la Révolution » (II, 4). Avec tout cet héritage de libre examen, il « frémit en songeant quel chrétien il ferait ». Il se rappelle son enfance, l'influence

qu'eurent sur son imagination les figures
des dieux antiques, découvertes dans un
livre et plus vénérables à ses yeux que
« les pauvres images chrétiennes de l'église » ;
il évoque les enseignements de son oncle,
pour qui Dieu, c'était le soleil, la piété
d'une de ses tantes, et la prédication d'un
Anglais qui lui avait fait lire le Nouveau
Testament. « Je ne cite ces détails, insiste-
t-il, que pour indiquer les causes d'une certaine irrésolution qui s'est souvent unie chez
moi à *l'esprit religieux le plus prononcé.* »
Et sans transition, dans une phrase que
nous avons déjà citée, mais qui prend
maintenant son sens exact, il donne *Aurélia* pour l'histoire du retour au « sentiment
précis de *diverses vérités* » que, « éloigné
longtemps de *la vraie route* », il n'avait pas
assez fermement recueillies (II, 4).

Ce texte capital ne souffre pas deux
interprétations : c'est bien des vérités
chrétiennes qu'il s'agit. C'est en elles qu'il
trouve une force à opposer au malheur, au
désespoir et au suicide, qui « sont le résultat
de certaines situations fatales pour qui
n'a pas foi dans l'immortalité, dans ses

peines et dans ses joies ». Si l'on en pouvait douter encore, les scènes suivantes seraient une confirmation éclatante. Une longue journée de vagabondage désespéré à travers Paris et les terrains vagues de la barrière de Clichy l'amène enfin rue de la Victoire, où il rencontre un prêtre ; il lui demande d'entendre sa confession et, comme le prêtre ne peut l'écouter avant le lendemain, il s'en va en pleurant à Notre-Dame de Lorette, où il implore de la Vierge le pardon de ses fautes. Il raconte de façon profondément émouvante le sacrifice symbolique qu'il fit alors de ses attaches orientales et la bouleversante impression que produisit sur lui le sermon :

« J'allai me mettre à genoux aux dernières places du chœur, et je fis glisser de mon doigt une bague d'argent dont le chaton portait gravés ces trois mots arabes : Allah ! Mohamed ! Ali ! Aussitôt plusieurs bougies s'allumèrent dans le chœur, et l'on commença un office auquel je tentai de m'unir en esprit. Quand on en fut à l'*Ave Maria*, le prêtre s'interrompit au milieu de l'oraison et recommença sept

fois sans que je pusse retrouver dans ma
mémoire les paroles suivantes. On termina
ensuite la prière, et le prêtre fit un discours
qui me semblait faire allusion à moi seul.
Quand tout fut éteint, je me levai et je
sortis... »

L'instant de la délivrance n'est pas
venu encore. Les paroles du prêtre, tout
cet office que Gérard a pu croire célébré
à sa seule intention, n'ont fait que rendre
plus intense le sentiment de la faute irré-
parable et de la malédiction. L'idée du
suicide reparaît, et le paysage parisien,
comme si souvent chez le Nerval d'*Aurélia*
et des *Nuits d'octobre*, se métamorphose
en un paysage symbolique, où les jeux de
la lumière et de l'ombre concrétisent le
tourment intérieur. Une vision d'Apocalypse se déroule ; un soleil noir, et un
globe rouge sang sur les Tuileries annon-
cent le début de la nuit éternelle ; la terre
sortie de son orbite erre parmi des lunes
multiples. Nerval rentre à l'aube ; au
réveil, il est étonné de revoir la lumière
et d'entendre un chœur mystérieux de
voix enfantines répéter : *Christe ! Christe !*

Christe ! « Mais le Christ n'est plus ; ils ne le savent pas encore ! » se dit-il, persistant à associer les visions de lumière et de ténèbres à son angoisse religieuse. Ce fut ce matin-là que Nerval échoua chez Heine, qui le fit conduire à la maison de santé.

Sorti de clinique au bout d'un mois, il se met à errer de nouveau dans Paris, courant de Montmartre au Luxembourg, des Tuileries aux Halles, tournant autour de Saint-Eustache. Un jour, il y entre, s'agenouille à l'autel de la Vierge en pensant à sa mère et, en sortant, achète un anneau d'argent, qui prend symboliquement la place de la bague orientale. Arrivé au Jardin des Plantes, et surpris par la pluie, il croit assister au déluge ; mais il jette son anneau dans les flots et de nouveau le paysage subit une transfiguration qui reflète les événements intérieurs. « Vers le même moment l'orage s'apaisa, et un rayon de soleil commença à briller. L'espoir rentra dans mon âme. » (II,5.)

Pourtant, à Passy où il est de nouveau interné, la tentation magique et les anciennes croyances « syncrétiques » de

Gérard résistent à l'envahissement des images chrétiennes. Il se croit la mission de rétablir l'harmonie universelle « en évoquant les forces occultes des diverses religions » II, 6). Il s'enivre de la vision d'un univers de secrètes correspondances. Mais, en pleine extase panthéiste, il s'arrête : la Mort elle-même, dans une pareille conception du monde, serait impuissante à nous affranchir, « car nous revivons dans nos fils comme nous avons vécu dans nos pères ». Qu'est-ce donc qu'une religion qui ne répond pas à ce besoin d'une immortalité bienheureuse qu'il sent en lui ? Les esprits hostiles ne nous ont-ils pas emprisonnés dans cet ordre définitif des générations successives et des réincarnations infinies ? N'est-ce pas pire qu'une éternelle damnation ?

Une fois encore, à ce nouvel échafaudage de son esprit, monte en lui l'angoisse primitive, la crainte du Néant. La mort, si elle n'est pas une délivrance des liens terrestres, confère toute son horreur irrémédiable à « l'éternelle distinction du bon et du mauvais », qui est l'aspect méta-

physique de la hantise du Double. C'est
à cela qu'il faut se soustraire ; « déplacer
les conditions du bien et du mal », il l'avait
rêvé déjà, à l'époque où dans une vie de
voyages et de joyeux carnaval il cherchait
l'oubli de ses peines (I, 1). Maintenant, il
tente d'y parvenir encore, en parcourant
non plus le monde de la variété, du caprice,
des costumes exotiques, mais celui des
croyances ; et son esprit édifie les constructions les plus fragiles. Isis, la Vénus antique,
la Vierge des chrétiens se confondent encore
en une figure magique en laquelle il met
son espoir (II, 6). Il faudra la renaissance de
la pitié et l'épisode du jeune homme malade
pour qu'enfin les visions s'éclaircissent et
qu'y apparaisse le Messie, triomphateur
de la Mort, au milieu du cantique de la
terre entière chantant le pardon. Les
perles, les fleurs, les oiseaux entourent de
leur splendeur les chevauchées où « la
grande amie » entraîne Gérard.

« O Mort ! où est ta victoire, puisque le
Messie vainqueur chevauchait entre nous
deux ? Sa robe était d'hyacinthe soufrée,
et ses poignets, ainsi que les chevilles de

ses pieds, étincelaient de diamants et de rubis. Quand sa houssine légère toucha la porte de nacre de la Jérusalem nouvelle, nous fûmes tous les trois inondés de lumière...

« Je sors d'un rêve bien doux ; j'ai revu celle que j'avais aimée transfigurée et radieuse. Le ciel s'est ouvert dans toute sa gloire, et j'y ai lu le mot *pardon* signé du sang de Jésus-Christ. » (II, 7.)

Ce pardon n'est pas seulement celui de la faute qui hantait Gérard : il s'étend à tous, à l'Ennemi lui-même, au « dieu du Nord » qui a voulu écraser de son marteau la sainte table composée de sept métaux les plus précieux.

« Malheur à toi, dieu-forgeron, qui as voulu briser un monde ! — Cependant, le pardon du Christ a été aussi prononcé pour toi !... Le serpent qui entoure le Monde est béni lui-même, car il relâche ses anneaux, et sa gueule béante aspire la fleur d'anxoka, la fleur soufrée, — la fleur éclatante du soleil ! »

Le rêve, ainsi, proclame que le pardon du dieu chrétien finira par triompher de tous les esprits du mal, par réintégrer dans le ciel les maudits eux-mêmes. C'est sur ce mythe, qui n'est pas sans analogies avec les grandioses imaginations de Hugo dans la *Fin de Satan*, que s'achèvent les visions de Nerval ; un dernier songe le transporte à Vienne, puis sur la Néwa : les deux Catherine, l'impératrice sainte Hélène, les plus belles princesses de Moscovie et de Pologne, ont les regards tournés vers la France. « Je vis par là que notre patrie devenait l arbitre de la querelle orientale... Mon rêve se termina par le doux espoir que la paix nous serait enfin donnée. » (II, 8). Car il faut que l'apaisement enfin trouvé par Gérard soit accordé à tous les hommes.

Cette résolution des conflits, accomplie par le rêve, se communique à la vie réelle. Nerval le précise encore à la dernière page d'*Aurélia :* la conscience d'être purifié de ses fautes passées et la certitude de l'immortalité, qui lui est « arrivée matériellement, pour ainsi dire », sont les deux éléments qui désormais lui donnent « des jouissances morales infinies ».

Est-ce donc une œuvre chrétienne qu'*Au-

rélia, et peut-on aller jusqu'à interpréter comme une manière de conversion cet allégement auquel parvient Gérard de Nerval au terme de cette œuvre héroïque ? Il n'y a aucun doute : lui même le pensait, nous l'avons vu ; et l'on pourrait invoquer aussi cette préface d'un article sur *Quintus Aucler*, où il écrivait en 1851 :

« Il y a, certes, quelque chose de plus effrayant dans l'histoire que la chute des empires, c'est la mort des religions... S'il était vrai que la religion chrétienne n'eût guère plus d'un siècle à vivre encore, — ne faudrait-il pas s'attacher avec larmes et avec prières aux pieds sanglants de ce Christ détaché de l'arbre mystique, à la robe immaculée de cette Vierge mère, — expression suprême de l'alliance antique du ciel et de la terre, — dernier baiser de l'esprit divin qui pleure et qui s'envole ! »

Il serait facile, même, d'opposer aux mouvements de révolte de certaines des *Chimères*, « Antéros », « Delfica », et surtout « Arthémis » :

La sainte de l'abîme est plus sainte à mes yeux !

tel autre vers, de *El Desdichado*, par exemple :

> *Et j'ai deux fois vainqueur traversé l'Achéron :*
> *Modulant tour à tour sur la lyre d'Orphée*
> *Les soupirs de la sainte et les cris de la fée.*

où l'on peut croire que se trouve un écho des deux parties d'*Aurélia* et que, dans ce second sonnet, la fée, la sainte de l'abîme n'est plus préférée.

Mais il est bien périlleux d'introduire tant de logique dans le mythe d'ombre et de lumière où se débattit Nerval. Gardons-nous de ramener à des dogmes trop précis, à des idéologies bien conscientes ces images qui luttent en lui.

Il est évident que des *images* chrétiennes, en effet, dominent de plus en plus à mesure que se déroule le récit d'*Aurélia* ; évident aussi que le sentiment de charité qui provoque la certitude du pardon est d'inspiration chrétienne. On ne peut nier non plus qu'il y ait, dans certains épisodes, comme celui des deux anneaux, l'intention de renoncer aux erreurs « orientales » pour revenir au christianisme.

Mais il serait malaisé de faire concorder ce christianisme avec les dogmes orthodoxes : cette « conversion » est bien exceptionnelle, qui, plutôt qu'aux Saintes Écritures, confère une valeur de révélation à des rêves. A vrai dire, Nerval a triomphé successivement de toutes les tentations de révolte et de magie qui se sont présentées à lui ; il leur a opposé une vertu de résignation et une volonté admirables. Il a fini par accepter les épreuves de son existence et par mettre tout son effort à leur donner la signification cohérente d'une lente rédemption. N'est-il pas bien présomptueux, lorsqu'un homme soumis à de pareils tourments témoigne d'un aussi prodigieux héroïsme, d'aller lui demander compte de son orthodoxie et de la mesurer aux mesures ordinaires ? L'archevêque de Paris le savait bien, qui, sur la foi des déclarations du Dr Blanche, lui accorda, malgré son suicide, la sépulture chrétienne.

*
* *

C'est au rêve, disions-nous, que Nerval demande la révélation des vérités suprêmes.

Plutôt encore, c'est à un lien qu'il finit par percevoir entre le Rêve et la Vie. Mais pas davantage qu'à la conviction de son propre salut et de la victoire du Messie sur la Mort, il n'est parvenu sans effort à cette domination du rêve. Et c'est là une dernière courbe, que l'on peut suivre au long de l'œuvre et que Nerval souligne avec une insistance particulière, l'opposant sans cesse à l'idée d'un retour à la raison. Les dernières phrases sont très importantes à bien saisir, car de l'interprétation qu'on leur donne dépend celle de l'œuvre entière. Parlant de cet autre malade auquel il s'intéresse et qui se croit en purgatoire, Gérard conclut :

« Telles sont les idées bizarres que donnent ces sortes de maladies ; je reconnus en moi-même que je n'avais pas été loin d'une si étrange persuasion. Les soins que j'avais reçus m'avaient déjà rendu à l'affection de ma famille et de mes amis, et je pouvais juger plus sainement le monde d'illusions où j'avais quelque temps vécu. »

Voilà qui semble clair : guéri, Nerval

reconnaît que ses rêves et ses visions n'ont été que démence, et il renonce à toute ironie envers « ce qu'on est convenu d'appeler la raison ». Mais il y a une réserve, et d'importance :

« *Toutefois,* je me sens heureux des convictions que j'ai acquises, et je compare cette série d'épreuves que j'ai traversées à ce qui, pour les anciens, représentait l'idée d'une *descente aux enfers.* »

Du coup, nous voici sur un autre plan de conscience, où rêves et visions ne sont plus de bizarres illusions, dont, redevenu normal, on juge plus sainement ; d'une descente aux enfers, on rapporte des convictions absolument valables. Le rêve transforme la vie, en révèle la valeur la plus profonde. Le mot rêve, il est vrai, n'est pas prononcé ; mais on ne peut méconnaître le lien qui rattache cette phrase finale à la page précédente, et l'idée de la descente aux enfers à celle d'une plongée aux royaumes intérieurs du rêve.

« Je m'encourageais à une audacieuse tentative. Je résolus de fixer le rêve et d'en connaître le secret. — Pourquoi, me dis-je, ne point enfin forcer ces portes mystiques, armé de toute ma volonté, et dominer mes sensations au lieu de les subir ? N'est-il pas possible de dompter cette chimère attrayante et redoutable, d'imposer une règle à ces esprits des nuits qui se jouent de notre raison ? Le sommeil occupe le tiers de notre vie. Il est la consolation des peines de nos journées ou la peine de leurs plaisirs ; mais je n'ai jamais éprouvé que le sommeil fût un repos. Après un engourdissement de quelques minutes, *une vie nouvelle* commence, affranchie des conditions du temps et de l'espace, et *pareille sans doute à celle qui nous attend après la mort...* Dès ce moment, je m'appliquai à chercher le sens de mes rêves, et cette inquiétude influa sur mes réflexions de l'état de veille. Je crus comprendre qu'il existait entre le monde externe et le monde interne un lien... »

La valeur extraor inaire que Nerval accorde au rêve apparaît ici en toute netteté, avec ses aspects si divers : le rêve, c'est d'abord ce que l'on entend le plus couramment par là, les images du sommeil. Mais ces images constituent une autre vie, pleine de menaces et d'attraits, dans laquelle nous échappons aux conditions terrestres. Ce que nous y pouvons percevoir « dès à présent », c'est la préfiguration de la vie éternelle ; seulement, pour que les abîmes intérieurs prennent cette exceptionnelle portée, il faut en *forcer* les portes. Car, dans notre état habituel, ce monde, — que nous appellerions aujourd'hui le monde de l'inconscient, — ne nous apparaît pas dans toute sa pureté. « L'inattention ou le désordre d'esprit », poursuit Nerval, faussent les rapports des deux réalités, et ainsi s'explique « la bizarrerie de certains tableaux semblables à ces reflets grimaçants d'objets réels qui s'agitent sur l'eau troublée ».

Tout ceci témoigne d'une connaissance très immédiate, et saisie avec une merveilleuse sincérité, des relations entre les deux moitiés, diurne et nocturne, qui constituent ensemble la continuité de notre être. Mais on y perçoit encore une assimilation du monde des rêves à une réalité transcendante, assimilation qui est le résultat du long effort de Nerval pour substituer des croyances salutaires aux accidents de son existence. Ce n'est pas sans raison qu'il a encadré toute sa confession entre deux affirmations, à peine différentes, de cette croyance, dont il fait ainsi l'idée centrale de l'œuvre. Les premières phrases d'*Aurélia* le disent avec une étrange solennité :

« Le rêve est une seconde vie. Je n'ai pu percer sans frémir ces portes d'ivoire ou de corne qui nous séparent du *monde invisible*. Les premiers instants du sommeil sont l'image de la mort ; un engourdissement nébuleux saisit notre pensée, et nous ne pouvons déterminer l'instant précis où le « moi », sous une autre forme, *continue l'œuvre de l'existence*. C'est un souterrain vague qui s'éclaire peu à peu, et où se dégagent de l'ombre et de la nuit les pâles figures, gravement immobiles, qui habitent le séjour des limbes. Puis le tableau se forme, une clarté nouvelle illumine et fait jouer ces apparitions bizarres : — *le monde des Esprits s'ouvre pour nous.* »

Le mouvement qui a mené Nerval jus-

qu'à ces affirmations est exactement le
même que nous avons tenté de suivre sur
d'autres plans : ce grand rythme, celui du
récit d'*Aurélia*, commence par l'irruption,
passivement subie, de quelque chose qui
s'abat sur Gérard et va, d'infortune en
infortune, jusqu'à prendre entière possession de lui. Mais, à l'instant où il est sur
le point d'être terrassé, il a un geste de
révolte. Sa volonté se redresse, et toute
la seconde partie raconte la lutte de cette
volonté pour triompher, pour s'emparer de
ce qui s'emparait d'elle : jusqu'à la lumière
finale.

Les rêves et les visions (Nerval ne distingue pas toujours) de la première partie
marquent un progressif « épanchement du
songe dans la vie réelle » (I, 3) : tout prend
un aspect double, sans que la mémoire
perde jamais un détail ou que la logique
semble atteinte. Une continuité s'établit
entre les deux mondes, inquiétante et
inexplicable. Transporté dans des visions
agréables, Nerval y éprouve le regret de
son existence habituelle ; mais rentré dans
celle-ci, il se désole d'avoir laissé échapper

le paradis. Rêve et vie sont deux mondes entre lesquels se débat l'homme, également attiré vers l'un et vers l'autre. A l'état habituel, ces deux mondes sont séparés, et l'étrangeté commence dans le récit nervalien au moment précis où la cloison cesse d'être étanche. Angoissé d'abord, Nerval s'abandonne bientôt à l'espèce d'euphorie que lui donne ce passage facile d'un plan à l'autre.

« La seule différence pour moi de la veille au sommeil était que, dans la première, tout se transfigurait à mes yeux ; chaque personne qui m'approchait semblait changée, les objets matériels avaient comme une pénombre qui en modifiait la forme, et les jeux de lumière, les combinaisons des couleurs se décomposaient, de manière à m'entretenir dans une série constante d'impressions qui se liaient entre elles, et dont le rêve, plus dégagé des éléments extérieurs, continuait la probabilité. » (I, 3.)

Puis, la différence entre les deux mondes lui redevient perceptible ; mais, bien loin de s'en réjouir, il en souffre. Au cœur du rêve, la conscience de la rechute prochaine dans l'autre réalité le blesse. La fissure béante qui sépare les deux moitiés de la vie n'a plus son aspect normal. Ce sentiment s'accroît après les rêves où il puise la certitude de l'immortalité future. Désormais, il n'est plus séparé de ceux qu'il aima que par les heures du jour, et il « attend celles de la nuit dans une douce mélancolie » (I, 5).

A l'instant du grand désespoir, lorsqu'il croit avoir offensé la mémoire d'Aurélia, il interroge le sommeil : mais le rêve répond par des images sanglantes, par l'apparition du double et par une liaison toujours plus frappante avec les événements de la veille. Gérard ne songe pas à ces explications que l'on trouve ordinairement toutes simples et qui admettent que le rêve compose ses scènes d'éléments réels conservés par la mémoire : la logique différente qui est déjà la sienne l'amène à d'autres conclusions, qui partent de cette conviction que le monde de l'imagination est aussi réel que l'autre : « Je ne sais comment expliquer que, dans mes idées, les événements terrestres pouvaient coïncider avec ceux du monde surnaturel, cela est plus facile à *sentir* qu'à énoncer clairement » (I, 9). Il devine bien ici que son évidence immédiate n'est pas la même que l'évidence logique ; et désormais toutes les démarches de son esprit vont procéder de ces intuitions directes.

Puisque le monde des rêves est réel et que nous y touchons à une sphère qui est celle de l'immortalité, Nerval se donne pour tâche de rejoindre, dès maintenant, tout ce que le rêve pourra lui livrer de l'Au-delà. A la passivité qui l'avait fait assister au spectacle des rêves, succédera l'effort de conquête.

« J'employai toutes les forces de ma *volonté* pour pénétrer encore le mystère dont j'avais levé quelques voiles. Le rêve se jouait parfois de mes efforts et n'*amenait* que des figures grimaçantes et fugitives. » (I,10.)

Toute la seconde partie est sous le signe de cette décision de l'emporter, de descendre aux abîmes du rêve pour en rapporter les trésors : « Avec cette idée que je m'étais faite du rêve comme ouvrant à l'homme une communication avec le monde des esprits, j'espérais,... j'espérais encore ». Mais les premiers songes de cette époque sont sombres, pleins de fatales apparitions et d'avertissements désespérants. De plus en plus, les mêmes colorations se répandent sur la vie éveillée et sur le rêve : cauchemars sanglants et incursions dans des villes merveilleuses ou des jardins délicieux alternent, commandant la succession des épouvantes et des espoirs. Tous les événements décisifs, annonce du pardon, venue du Messie, se passent en rêve. Mais pour finir, — et c'est là le signe du triomphe, — ce qui est obtenu en rêve est assuré pour la vie éveillée aussi. Toutes les certitudes et les promesses acquises dans l'univers spirituel, désormais lumineux, le sont également pour le monde terrestre où Gérard redescend, apaisé.

*
* *

Victoire bien illusoire, dit-on, puisque, avant même d'avoir revu toutes les épreuves d'*Aurélia*, Gérard Labrunie, dit de Nerval, était trouvé pendu, en habit et en chapeau noirs, pantalon gris-vert et guêtres grises, dans la sinistre impasse de la Vieille-Lanterne où il avait échoué une nuit de janvier, après des journées de lamentables pérégrinations. Repris par la folie ? abandonné par la confuse exaltation qui lui avait dicté les trompeuses rêveries de cette *Aurélia*, destinée à démontrer qu'il n'était pas fou ? Ou bien, — puisqu'il avait réussi à sortir de Passy dans le dessein avoué de refaire sa réputation littéraire, — vaincu par l'impossibilité d'écrire, par la misère, la peur de la déchéance matérielle ?

Non, tout cela est trop simple, trop près de ce qui peut arriver à n'importe qui, trop selon la logique. Ce qui s'est passé réellement, on ne le saura jamais, mais il est certain que cela ne correspondit à aucune des démarches de l'esprit que nous sommes capables de reconstituer. Et, — ce qui compte davantage, — cette catastrophe ne saurait infirmer en rien la valeur d'*Aurélia* et l'authenticité de la victoire remportée. Les certitudes acquises, conquises sur la maladie, sur le rêve, sur la vie normale, qui nous prouve que Nerval ne les a pas gardées, intactes, au moment de son geste, que nous appelons « désespéré » ?

L'œuvre est là, et continue à porter témoignage comme elle le ferait si elle nous était parvenue sans que nous sachions rien de son auteur. Car elle nous parle le langage de la poésie ; si elle est convaincante, c'est par toute cette musique qui est en elle, par les trésors de tout ordre qu'elle renferme et que cent lectures n'épuisent pas plus que la prose de Rimbaud ne perd de son dur éclat à être sans cesse reprise. Cela ne veut pas dire, — bien au contraire ! — qu'il y ait dans ce genre d'œuvres une beauté de « forme », toute « littéraire », que l'on puisse admirer en dépit d'autre chose, qui en serait le « contenu ». Précisément, dans ces œuvres faites d'illuminations intérieures, la beauté que l'on y admire vient de ce que tout fait allusion à une réalité infiniment mystérieuse, mais infiniment réelle : et cette réalité ne prouve pas autrement sa présence que par le charme inépuisable qu'exerce la musique allusive des mots.

Entre Nerval et Rimbaud, en effet, il y a

plus de ressemblances qu'il ne peut paraître d'abord. Certes, l'aventure est très différente de l'adolescent que bouleverse une brusque illumination poétique, et de ce quadragénaire amené à créer, à la veille de sa mort, une œuvre que rien n'annonçait dans ses écrits déjà volumineux. Mais la « saison en enfer » de l'un, la « descente aux enfers » de l'autre présentent bien des analogies, ne serait-ce que dans cette ambition de conquérir des pouvoirs exceptionnels, et dans les doutes, les remords, la crainte d'être maudits pour avoir osé soulever le voile du mystère. « Je voulais trop faire en bravant la mort », a écrit Nerval. Et Rimbaud a renoncé à sa tentative angélique « parce que c'était mal ».

L'un et l'autre aussi ont découvert qu'il est une méthode, une espèce d'ascèse nécessaire à la conquête de la poésie telle qu'ils l'entendaient : au « je veux être poète et je travaille à me faire voyant » de Rimbaud, correspond ce fragment, plus humble de ton, que Nerval égara dès 1844 dans une revue :

« Je ne demande pas à Dieu de rien

changer aux événements, mais de me changer relativement aux choses ; de me laisser le pouvoir de créer autour de moi un univers qui m'appartienne, de *diriger mon rêve éternel au lieu de le subir.* »

Et surtout ce passage des manuscrits d'*Aurélia* :

« Il ne faut pas offenser la pudeur des divinités du songe. Il faut s'entretenir d'idées pures et saines pour avoir des songes logiques. Prenez garde à l'impureté qui effarouche les bons esprits et qui attire les divinités fatales. *Quand vos rêves sont logiques, ils sont une porte ouverte, ivoire ou corne, sur le monde extérieur...* »

C'est là que l'on saisit le véritable sens de cette confiance dans les rêves qu'avait Nerval : il y voyait un moyen de découverte : non seulement de découverte de soi-même, mais de connaissance de l'ultime réalité. C'est là une attitude romantique, plus proche d'ailleurs du romantisme allemand que du romantisme français. Dépassant le stade du subjectivisme qui n'est qu'expression lyrique, épanchement, confession de sentiments personnels, il descend en lui-même jusqu'aux « enfers », jusqu'à ces régions les plus profondes, les plus centrales, où le mystique atteint enfin à la seule réalité. Le rêve est l'un des moyens en notre pouvoir qui permettent d'échapper à la conscience de l'individu clos sur lui-même. « Toute descente en soi, a dit Novalis, tout regard à l'intérieur de nous-mêmes, est en même temps essor vers le ciel, regard vers le *véritable monde extérieur*. »

Ceux qui se risquent à ces profondeurs en ramènent ces œuvres singulières et durables qui conservent de leur auteur, non point son être accidentel et périssable, mais son essence et sa figure mythique. Ces explorations ne sont pas sans péril, car celui qui s'y aventure s'engage tout entier : l'œuvre se confond avec sa destinée elle-même, elle est le moyen par lequel il cherche à rejoindre cette région où se déroule, non plus sa propre histoire terrestre, mais sa destinée éternelle. Comme le mystique, il paie de l'anéantissement de sa personne cette plongée dans la nuit.

Et dès lors, il n'y a rien de surprenant

à ce que ces œuvres précisément agissent
sur nous avec cette séduction particulière,
« magique », inépuisable. Chaque phrase
en est un piège tendu, qui retient prisonnier
un fragment de cet univers dont nous
savons tous qu'il existe, mais dont les
échos ne nous parviennent que dans certains rêves ou dans la sorcellerie poétique.
Les magiciens qui captent ces échos
obéissent à des règles toutes particulières,
qui leur imposent un souci infini de la
forme : car rien n'est plus précis qu'un
rite magique.

Ces poètes ne choisissent pas leurs mots
ou leurs images selon quelque loi d'intelli-
gibilité dont ils seraient convenus avec
le commun des mortels : ils élisent ces
sonorités et ces allusions, pour eux-mêmes
intraduisibles, qui éveillent en eux les
ondes infinies d'une émotion révélatrice :
ce sera telle fleur, telle couleur, tel nom
de dieu, ou même telle syllabe, qu'une
association avec le souvenir tout personnel
d'un instant favorisé chargera pour eux
d'une valeur affective. Pour eux seuls,
semble-t-il d'abord ; mais s'ils sont de

vrais magiciens et s'ils suivent en toute
sincérité ces sortes de chocs intérieurs
que font en tout homme certaines images,
le miracle se produira et le lecteur *saura*
que le poème lui parle d'une réalité profonde.

Les sonnets de Nerval, dont lui-même
écrivait qu'ils « perdraient de leur charme
à être expliqués, *si la chose était possible* »,
sont les plus beaux exemples de cette
poésie. De patientes recherches ont pu en
retrouver les éléments dans la biographie
ou dans les lectures du poète ; mais toutes
les tentatives d'intrusion logique sont
restées vaines, car nul ne peut savoir exactement ce qui rendait chacun de ces éléments irremplaçable ; Nerval lui-même
n'eût su le dire, et pourtant le symbolisme
authentique de ces poèmes éveille en nous
des échos infinis.

La Treizième revient... C'est encor la première ;
Et c'est toujours la seule, — ou c'est le seul moment ;
Car es-tu reine, ô toi ! la première ou dernière ?
Es-tu roi, toi le seul ou le dernier amant ?

Aimez qui vous aima du berceau dans la bière ;
Celle que j'aimai seul m'aime encor tendrement :

C'est la mort — ou la morte... O délice ! ô tourment !
La rose qu'elle tient, c'est la Rose trémière.

Sainte napolitaine aux mains pleines de feux,
Rose au cœur violet, fleur de sainte Gudule :
As-tu trouvé ta croix dans le désert des cieux ?

Roses blanches, tombez ! vous insultez nos dieux !
Tombez, fantômes blancs, de votre ciel qui brûle :
— La sainte de l'abîme est plus sainte à mes yeux !

Mais la prose de Nerval n'est pas moins magique. Je n'imagine pas que l'on puisse lire sans une émotion infinie certaines pages de *Sylvie*, ou une simple phrase comme celle-ci, dont le symbolisme de couleurs exerce un attrait qui défie toute analyse :

« Cet amour vague et sans espoir, conçu pour une femme de théâtre, qui tous les soirs me prenait à l'heure du spectacle, pour ne me quitter qu'à l'heure du sommeil, avait son germe dans le souvenir d'Adrienne, fleur de la nuit éclose à la pâle clarté de la lune, fantôme rose et blond glissant sur l'herbe verte à demi baignée de blanches vapeurs. »

Ou ce fragment de *Pandora* :

« A ce spectacle succédèrent des apparitions fantastiques, images des dieux souterrains. La salle était tendue de rouge et des rosaces de diamant noir éclataient aux lueurs de l'ombre. »

Presque toutes les visions d'*Aurélia*, lugubres ou splendides, celle des lunes innombrables et errantes sur les Tuileries, comme celle de la descente à travers la terre en fusion, appartiennent à cette poésie miraculeuse. Mais rien n'est plus extraordinaire que l'allégresse de l'univers à l'apparition du Messie :

« Du sein des ténèbres muettes, deux notes ont résonné, l'une grave, l'autre aiguë, — et l'orbe éternel s'est mis à tourner aussitôt. Sois bénie, ô première Octave qui commença l'hymne divin ! Du dimanche au dimanche, enlace tous les jours dans ton réseau magique. Les monts te chantent aux vallées, les sources aux rivières, les rivières aux fleuves, et les fleuves à l'Océan ; l'air vibre, et la lumière baise harmonieusement les fleurs naissantes. Un soupir, un frisson d'amour sort du sein gonflé de la terre, et le chœur des astres se déroule dans l'infini ; il

s'écarte et revient sur lui-même, se resserre
et s'épanouit, et sème au loin les germes
des créations nouvelles. »

On ne sait ce qu'il y a, dans ces images
et dans ces mots sans originalité frappante,
qui s'élève, prend des ailes et fait comme
une danse aérienne. Jusque dans certaines
lettres de la démence, à jamais inexplicables, des phrases éclatent comme celle-ci :
« Il fait si beau que l'on ne peut se ren-
contrer ni s'embrasser dans les maisons »
(à quoi fait un bien étrange écho Nietzsche
fou qui « aurait aimé à serrer dans ses bras
et à embrasser tous les gens dans la rue, et
à grimper jusqu'en haut des maisons »).
Ou encore ce billet qu'il écrivait à sa tante
l'avant-veille de sa mort : « Ne m'attends
pas ce soir, car la nuit sera noire et blanche ».
La nuit, la voici encore dans un fragment
de poème :

Quand un vent parfumé nous apporte en sa plainte
Quelques sons affaiblis d'une ancienne complainte,
O les feux du couchant vermeil, capricieux,
Montent comme un chemin splendide vers les cieux.
Il semble que Dieu dise à mon âme souffrante :
Quitte le monde impur, la foule indifférente,

Suis d'un pas assuré cette route qui luit,
Et viens à moi, mon fils — et n'attends pas LA NUIT.

**

La preuve dernière que donne de son authenticité, de sa « réalité » absolue, une œuvre telle qu'*Aurélia*, c'est sa résistance à toute exégèse. On peut y tracer des lignes, y suivre l'entremêlement de certains thèmes, et puis reprendre la lecture : le charme est intact, le mystère entier. Le profanateur, qui a voulu y saisir des idées, se retrouve devant le monde autrement profond des images, sirènes éternelles dont il suit l'appel vers les paysages mouvants du rêve, où tout prépare la venue d'une aurore promise.

POÉSIE ET MYSTIQUE

...Fût-ce au creux de la main fatale de la nuit.

HUGO.

Dès le romantisme, mais en toute conscience depuis Rimbaud, la poésie française tend à assimiler sa démarche à un acte de connaissance irrationnelle. L'esthétique qui s'est lentement élaborée, à travers le symbolisme et le surréalisme, présente ceci de nouveau qu'elle attribue nettement à l'art une efficacité toute proche de celle que l'on reconnaît aux pouvoirs magiques, aux efforts mystiques, et aux contemplations de l'esprit spéculatif. On peut se demander, d'ailleurs, si cette ambition est vraiment nouvelle, et si la poésie n a pas toujours été, en un certain sens, une exploration de cet ordre : il ne nous est guère possible, en tout cas (faut-il

croire qu'une illusion se joue de nous et
nous fait miroiter ces ressemblances ?),
de ne pas apercevoir chez les poètes antiques
eux-mêmes une série de procédés et d'effets,
qui semblent bien viser à dominer quelque
réalité au delà du monde sensible. Leurs
intentions immédiatement reconnaissables
et avouées ne suffisent point à expliquer
l'art des classiques : une fois que l'on a
distingué, dans leurs œuvres, ce qui appartient à la déclamation de l'amphithéâtre
et qui se propose d'agir sur un public de
citoyens réunis, il demeure une matière
poétique proprement inexplicable, dont
ne rendra compte aucune analyse des
moyens employés. Qu'il s'agisse de l'épopée ionienne, ou de la tragédie attique,
de l'art racinien ou du lyrisme romantique,
la narration épique, la figure morale des
héros, l'intelligence ou l'aveu des événements affectifs n'atteignent pas encore à
ce qui fait le pouvoir de durée de toutes
ces œuvres : l'action d'une musique partout
présente. Tout cela, en quoi nous recon-
naissons la particularité des époques et
des civilisations successives, peut vieillir,

les guerriers de Troie être aussi différents de nous qu'un homme parvient à l'être d'un autre homme, les problèmes rituels d'*Œdipe à Colone* échapper à notre esprit, la vérité psychologique des personnages raciniens ignorer certains abîmes familiers à notre introspection : le charme n'agit pas moins sur nous de ces œuvres dont l'immortalité doit bien consister en *autre chose* que leurs éléments susceptibles de vieillissement.

Des études, encore très incomplètes, sur la technique poétique nous enseignent déjà que ce surplus toujours efficace se compose apparemment de souplesse ou de variété prosodique, de rapports de couleurs ou de nombres, de moyens allusifs ; or justement, cela n'explique rien et nous indique simplement que la magie poétique recourt à des sensations dont l'effet est certain, mais ne se ramène pas à ces sensations elles-mêmes. La poésie fait, de ces éléments simples et mesurables, mètres, rythmes, sonorités, un usage qui reste entièrement mystérieux. On n'a point éclairci pourquoi la variété et la sûreté des formes rythmiques provoquait l'euphorie, pourquoi l'évocation d'une chose par une couleur symbolique était plus émouvante que la désignation claire de cette chose. L'association d'images habituellement lointaines leur confère soudain une qualité qui n'est plus tout à fait la qualité de l'objet évoqué. L'esprit se sent comme une liberté souveraine, — qui n'appartient réellement qu'au poète, inventeur du bond et de la métaphore, mais dont la sensation obscure se communique à l'esprit du lecteur.

Il n'est pas possible, sans doute, dans l'état où en est restée notre connaissance des réactions esthétiques, de définir plus exactement cette singulière harmonie qui, miraculeusement établie entre un rythme verbal et un rythme intérieur, entre une image poétique et le brusque transfert de l'être sur un plan de réalité tout particulier, provoque en nous une certitude profonde : la certitude de communiquer soudain avec quelque chose de réel, d'*autrement* réel. Comment se fait-il, par exemple, que dans l'*Agamemnon* d'Eschyle la couleur rouge, sans cesse suggérée par la langue et par les tapis étendus sous les pieds du guerrier rentrant chez lui, suffise à créer cette angoisse qui prépare la scène sanglante ? Et comment se fait-il que cette suggestion par l'image, suscitant chez nous un choc singulier, soit précisément ce que nous appelons la poésie d'Eschyle ? Ce choc, qui se produit en une région de nous-mêmes inaccessible à la conscience et laissée dans l'ombre par la vie quotidienne, il est tout naturel qu'il nous apparaisse comme le signe d'un événement intérieur de la plus haute importance.

Et pourtant, il subsiste, entre cette action du poète ancien et celle à laquelle vise le poète moderne, une différence. La poésie post-romantique n'a point une autre essence que la poésie éternelle, — sinon à quoi reconnaîtrions-nous qu'elle est encore poésie ? — mais elle a pris une assez nette conscience de sa nature. Son action a cessé d'être entièrement obscure, pour le poète comme pour le lecteur ; l'un et l'autre demandent à l'art une révélation, et, s'ils ne peuvent donner les raisons de

cet espoir, ils en connaissent l'existence.
Nous trouvons chez les anciens bien peu
de textes qui affirment la valeur de l'acte
poétique. Mais il est imprudent d'en
conclure qu'ils ignoraient tout de la portée
que nous lui conférons. Socrate se méfiait
des poètes dans la mesure justement où
ils étaient impuissants à expliquer leurs
œuvres, où ils déclenchaient des explosions dont ils ignoraient le secret et ne
pouvaient fournir la justification théorique.

Tel est donc le paradoxe de la poésie
moderne : elle se veut abandonnée aux
automatismes et aux dictées de l'inconscient, mais elle est de plus en plus
consciente de cette volonté. Elle reste
ignorante de la portée de ses gestes, car il
est probable que ceux-ci ne sont efficaces
que protégés par cette ignorance ; mais
elle sait qu'elle accomplit un acte incalculable, elle sait qu'il lui faut faire confiance
à certaines pratiques, sans en connaître
le sens. Elle tente d'atteindre, par delà la
connaissance rationnelle qu'a lentement
acquise l'humanité, une communication
directe, intuitive, avec les choses, qui est

celle des primitifs ; mais ce retour aux pouvoirs originels ne peut s'accomplir qu'à la lumière des pouvoirs conquis.

C'est par ce paradoxe que se définit la particularité de la poésie nouvelle, et non point par son usage du symbole, qui est celui de toute poésie. Et toutes les caractéristiques que l'on en peut donner s'appliquent de même à la tentative poétique de tous les temps, avec cette seule et essentielle différence qu'il y faut joindre, chez le poète actuel, une claire conscience de tout ce que le poète ancien possédait également, mais sans s'en rendre compte.

*
* *

Les caractères par lesquels on a défini récemment l'essence de la poésie ont amené bien des esprits à se demander s'il n'y avait pas identité absolue, ou tout au moins convergence profonde, entre les démarches du poète et du mystique.

L'exploration des profondeurs psychiques et des régions obscures de l'être est apparue comme possible par la voie de l'expression poétique. Le poète semble être celui qui fait confiance à certaines associations, pour lui-même inexplicables, choisies parce qu'elles appellent en lui un assentiment irraisonné. Mots en liberté, écriture automatique, tant de tentatives récentes reposent sur une croyance qui appartient à la tradition occultiste : croyance en une analogie profonde entre la nature extérieure et la structure du monde intérieur. Telle opération spontanée de notre esprit, accomplie dans ces régions inconscientes où n'intervient aucune faculté d'ordonnance ou de construction logique, doit nécessairement correspondre à tel événement naturel ou cosmique. Dès lors, chaque groupe de mots issu des profondeurs incontrôlées doit nécessairement saisir un aspect, un fragment de ce réel, qui est en nous aussi bien que hors de nous. Sa réalité se trahit, non point par quelque consentement universel, mais par une sensation d'ineffable présence, d'évidence concrète. Et Paul Éluard dit magnifiquement que la poésie est « l'appel des choses par leur nom ».

Ainsi se forme l'étrange espoir d'atteindre, précisément par le subjectivisme absolu, à la seule objectivité valable : c'est au terme de la descente en soi, alors qu'il n'accepte plus que ce qui est unique et personnel, que l'homme prétend saisir enfin quelque chose qui le dépasse. Il veut à la fois épanouir tous ses pouvoirs, intégrer dans l'acte essentiel les instincts et les automatismes, et en même temps écarter de lui ce qui est intellectuel uniquement. Ainsi arrive-t-il à cette poésie dont les manifestations ont quelque ressemblance avec les produits de l'âme primitive ; tout y est correspondance entre des plans que dissocie l'analyse intellectuelle, toute chose y est animée, et semble être à l'état de perpétuelle naissance. Poésie du monde en formation et de l'être en formation, où transparaît sans cesse une nostagie, l'appel de l'âme vers un paradis perdu, vers l'âge d'or primitif, que connaissent tous les mythes. Poésie de l'enfance, du rêve, du souvenir, semblable à un ciel immense où les nuages dessinent des formes fugitives.

Les diverses démarches de cet esprit poétique sont apparemment et logiquement inconciliables : les mêmes poètes qui se livrent aux inspirations de la nuit intérieure, recherchent une consonance étroite avec toutes les fuyantes apparitions du monde visible. Niant la réalité de l'univers extérieur, ils semblent aspirer à la fois à ne plus baigner que dans leur propre substance psychique, et à se dégager des limites du moi pour s'abandonner aux instables figures que le hasard et l'instant forment avec les choses.

Mais la contradiction n'est que de surface. Toutes ces démarches se ramènent bien à un seul et même geste fondamental, qui est d'attribuer un pouvoir de découverte à l'acte même de créer le poème, d'associer librement les images, et de faire jaillir la métaphore. Au delà de tous ces abandons à la multiplicité des figures de l'esprit et à la variété inépuisable des formes et des choses, le propos du poète est de rejoindre l'unité essentielle : unité de l'esprit et du monde, cherchée passionnément, pathétiquement, aussi bien dans la contemplation du spectacle extérieur que dans l'appréhension des données obscures du monde profond.

Cette recherche de l'unité donne à l'image, à la métaphore, une double fonction : elle sert, d'une part, par l'accumulation même des images les plus disparates, à opérer une sorte de destruction de l'univers sensible ; l'esprit, entraîné dans ce tourbillon, ne peut se fixer sur aucun objet, et tous ceux qui sont évoqués, par de rapides allusions, ne le sont qu'en fonction de quelque autre chose, d'innommé et d'ineffable, vers quoi s'oriente peu à peu le poète. Mais, d'autre part, l'image tend à saisir, pour autant que cela est possible, cette présence concrète d'un au-delà du moi, cette évidence d'une région de nous-mêmes plus profonde que nous. Elle cherche à coïncider, d'aussi près qu'il se pourra, avec ces naissances intérieures et ces formations chaotiques de l'inconscient, en lesquelles on se plaît à reconnaître les fragments d'une autre réalité.

Le poète s'abandonne, attentif, à ce double flot des images : celles qui lui viennent du spectacle environnant, par une sorte de vertige, ôtent sa réalité au monde sensible, le rendent transparent, l'assimilent à un système de symboles qui signifient davantage qu'eux-mêmes. Et les autres, celles qui montent des profondeurs de l'être, s'accordent finalement à ces symboles, composent avec eux un chant qui parle d'un au-delà du réel, évoque le paradis de l'unité primitive, et redit à l'âme ses mystérieuses appartenances. Au sommet de l'expérience poétique, les frontières entre un monde extérieur et un monde intérieur s'abattent ; tout est image offerte à la libre disposition d'un esprit qui recompose à sa guise l'ordonnance de toutes les données. Il en refait un univers à sa convenance, selon son plaisir, en se conformant aux seules lois de cette euphorie que suscite en lui tel rythme, tel écho sonore, telle association de formes ou de couleurs. Mais, souverain, l'esprit cesse de se considérer comme l'auteur du chant où il trouve sa félicité : il lui semble percevoir une voix qui n'est plus la sienne. Ce qui parle, ce n'est plus lui, mais un autre, qui « fait son remuement dans les profondeurs », en une symphonie qui répond à son coup d'archet.

Dans la poésie récente, cette orientation de tout l'être vers une réalité qui dépasse la réalité extérieure et la détruit par sa présence même, a pris souvent un aspect singulier : celui de la mystification. Le poète, qui dispose des choses et qui en fait un usage très particulier, est amené à considérer avec ironie l'ordre habituel du monde. Parvenu à ce stade de conscience le plus profond où il rejoint le primitivisme, il ne trouve plus nulle part de contradiction logique : tout ce que notre raison oppose entre pour lui dans une harmonie qui est convergence vers le même foyer unique. Mais, de ce point de vue, les conventions et les distinctions de notre connaissance « normale » perdent pour lui toute gravité, et il se livre volontiers au jeu qui les brouille, les déplace, en souligne l'inconsistance. Le mot *mystifier* retrouve alors, de façon assez imprévue, son sens étymologique : les choses, brusquement groupées selon des lois informulables, qui sont celles de l'accident extérieur ou d'on ne sait quels coq-à-l'âne de l'inconscient, sont véritablement arrachées à leur signification banale, quotidienne, et *mysti-fiées*, redevenues libres et susceptibles d'assumer leur sens mystérieux, irrationnel. Au double rôle de l'image correspond ainsi le double sens du mot mystification : ce qui est mystifié, c'est à la fois, dans l'acception courante, la « réalité », le multiple, qu'une ironie transcendante anéantit par le jeu, — et à la fois, dans le sens littéral, les incalculables révélations de l'inconscient, ouvertures fugitives sur l'unité essentielle, avertissements témoignant d'une présence authentique.

Sous tous ces aspects divers de la poésie moderne, consciente de ses intentions, on peut distinguer la nature de toute aventure poétique : partant à la fois des choses et des données inconscientes, le poète aboutit à un état particulier, où toutes les contradictions logiques s'effacent, où se dessine une appréhension de l'unité psychique et cosmique, où le moi paraît s'évanouir pour céder la place à une voix qui parle à travers lui. Et cet état de poésie trouve son expression dans l'image, destructrice d'une réalité superficielle et témoin d'une réalité profonde ; dans le jeu aussi, qui est une autre forme de la sorcellerie. Tout au fond, le poète n'élève pas une moindre prétention que celle d'accomplir une opération souveraine et d'atteindre au concret.

**

Appel à l'unité, — descente aux régions où le moi se renonce en faveur d'une présence qu'il perçoit en lui, — action efficace de l'image : on ne peut se défendre d'abord de constater de singulières ressemblances entre ces définitions et celles qu'il est possible de donner de la mystique.

Pour le mystique aussi, le geste capital est la négation du multiple et l'affirmation de l'Un. Le chemin de perfection consiste à s'arracher au monde des apparences, au « samsara », et à s'élever jusqu'à la contemplation de l'unité. Deux itinéraires

y mènent, semblables aux deux voies de
la poésie, et comme elles convergents : le
chemin mystérieux qui, selon Novalis,
« va vers l'intérieur », aboutit à la même
union mystique que la contemplation de
l'unité à travers la fuyante multiplicité
des apparences. L'une et l'autre voie ache-
minent vers cet état de conscience où
s'efface toute contradiction, dans l'harmonie retrouvée, et où il semble que se
fasse entendre une voix étrangère au moi,
plus savante que lui, porteuse d'ineffables
secrets, qui « parle de l'intérieur » — *que
habla de dentro*, disait Saint-Jean de la
Croix.

L'analogie n'est pas moins frappante
en ce qui concerne le rôle des images :
celles auxquelles le mystique recourt, pour
évoquer dans la mesure du possible son
ineffable expérience, n'ont-elles pas pour
but premier de nous dire ce qu'il a éprouvé
au cours de sa plongée en soi ? et pour
seconde fonction, de nous présenter, soudain revêtu d'« être » sous la lumière de
l'unité contemplée, ce qui était d'abord
« samsara », néant des apparences ?

Enfin, ne peut-on trouver, chez le mystique comme chez le poète, l'intervention de l'ironie qui « mystifie » les objets, se raille de leur signification banale et les transporte sur un autre plan, où ils acquièrent une nouvelle transparence ? Cette ironie mystique se retrouve dans tous les poèmes d'amour qui, depuis le *Cantique des Cantiques*, semblent chanter la beauté terrestre, mais entendent suggérer une autre beauté, devant laquelle s'anéantit la première.

Et pourtant : ces définitions épuisent-elles bien toute la nature de l'expérience mystique ? L'analogie est-elle si parfaite qu'il faille effacer toute frontière entre la mystique et la poésie, et faire de celle-ci le vase privilégié des ambitions spirituelles ? Il est étrange, si poésie et mystique se confondent, ou même le peuvent à un stade idéal jamais atteint encore, que tous les poètes aient eu le sentiment de « ce grand échec qui se perpétue » et dont parlait jadis Aragon. De tout temps, le poète a eu, à de certains moments, l'impression d'être un maudit, un « voleur de feu », un être exposé par sa révolte à la colère divine. Le cas de Rimbaud n'est qu'un cas extrême, et on peut percevoir l'écho de ces mêmes orgueils et de ces mêmes craintes dans toute l'histoire de la poésie. En des instants de retour sur ses actes, ou de conversion religieuse, le poète en vient à s'accuser d'avoir cédé à la tentation d'angélisme. Pour s'être voulu innocent et libéré de la tache originelle, il croit être damné et il rejette avec horreur son œuvre : silence de Racine, angoisses de Baudelaire, remords de Nerval, — et soumission du Prométhée d'Eschyle, et fureurs de Platon législateur, qui s'acharne sur son passé de poète tragique... Le silence final du poète est un silence de vaincu qui se résigne ; celui du mystique est la paix de qui a atteint au terme de son aventure.

Il convient de reprendre les définitions que nous avons accepté d'appliquer à la mystique et qui correspondaient trop bien à celles qui sont justifiées pour la poésie : elles sont loin de circonscrire l'expérience mystique avec assez d'exactitude.

Et d'abord, le rôle de l'image : tandis

que la poésie ne peut renoncer à l'image sans cesser d'être, l'expression imagée disparaît chez le mystique, pour faire place au silence, lorsqu'il atteint au sommet de son ascension. Des deux degrés que distingue la théologie mystique, méditation et contemplation, seul le premier (qui n'est que préparatoire) comporte la naissance et la succession des images. L'ascèse, les exercices, la concentration de la volonté sur un objet de méditation n'ont d'autre fin que de dépasser la méditation elle-même et d'ouvrir les demeures plus intérieures du « château de l'âme ». Et c'est à ce premier stade que l'image intervient, ainsi que dans ces états d'exaltation, d'intense activité émotive, où l'on voit trop souvent l'essentiel de la mystique. La progression vers l'état le plus dénudé, auquel tendent tous les mystiques, est décrite par eux comme une mort des images, un arrachement de l'âme, qui quitte les régions, déjà profondes, où l'image succède à l'idée, pour atteindre enfin à ce centre qui est la Nuit absolue. C'est là ce qu'exprime le Bienheureux Seuse, lorsqu'il recommande de *chasser les images par des images*, afin de contempler *cette signification qui est vide d'images elle-même* ; ou encore Maître Eckhart, qui se demande *quelle est l'opération que Dieu fait sans images dans le fond de l'âme*, et qui répond :

Je ne suis pas en état de le savoir. Car les facultés de l'âme humaine ne peuvent percevoir que par images. Et comme les images viennent toujours du dehors, cette opération suprême leur reste cachée. Et c'est là chose éminemment salutaire. Car le non-savoir la séduit et l'attire vers quelque chose de miraculeux, et elle se met à la chasse de ce quelque chose : elle sent bien, en effet, que cela est, mais ne sait pas ce que c'est. — *Plus tu es sans images* (dit-il ailleurs), *et plus tu es accessible à l'action de Dieu en toi* ; *plus tu es tourné vers toi-même et oublieux* (du dehors), *et plus tu es proche de Dieu.*

Même conseil encore chez Fénelon, qui recommande d'*aller toujours par le non-voir.*

Mais l'image intervient une seconde fois *après* l'union accomplie, lorsque le mystique recourt à l'expression lyrique pour décrire approximativement l'expérience cruciale ; celle-ci, en elle-même, ne peut être saisie par l'image, qui se borne à orienter l'esprit vers elle. Dans ce sens, l'image du mystique, devenu poète, est l'adhésion la plus parfaite possible (mais par définition imparfaite) à une réalité *connue :* de là vient l'incessant effort des mystiques pour « prouver ce qui est sans preuve » et pour « figurer ce qui est sans images ».

Ce rôle de l'image peut éclairer les deux voies de la mystique : descente en soi, et contemplation de l'Unité dans le multiple. La seconde ne saurait se confondre avec une marche procédant de l'inconnu au connu, comme celle du poète : pour un Saint-Jean de la Croix, il ne s'agit pas de *trouver Dieu dans les choses,* mais, au contraire, de partir de l'intuition massive de l'Unité, seule *connue* par une connaissance véritablement première, antérieure à tout chemin et à tout progrès ; et ensuite seulement, au terme et au retour de l'expérience, de retrouver les choses qu'il avait fallu d'abord nier et rejeter au néant. *Trouver les choses en Dieu,* les saisir en cet instant où « elles cessent d'être des apparences isolées pour s'absorber dans l'Être » et pour en recevoir l'existence, tel est le mouvement de « retour » qui est la véritable relation du mystique avec la beauté du monde.

Quant à la voie de la descente en soi, c'est sans doute le langage de Maître Eckhart qui en donne la notion la plus exacte : les images s'adressent aux facultés, qui ne sont que notre moi en tant que nous sommes créatures, que nous sommes néant. Le tréfonds de l'âme, le *Grund,* la *scintilla animae,* ce point qu'aucune image ne saurait déterminer et où se passe la naissance de Dieu en nous, cette âme la plus profonde ne perçoit pas par images. Et ce qui s'y passe est tout ineffable.

De part et d'autre, les deux voies aboutissent à ce que notre langage appelle l'abîme, à la *Nuit* qui est suprême clarté ; au terme comme au principe de toute expérience mystique se trouve l'Un, le réel, dont la contemplation nous fait concevoir notre existence séparée comme un pur non-être.

Tout ceci peut se résumer en une formule grossière, mais qui suffit à notre propos actuel : le mystique ne va pas du sensible à l'inconnu, il ne va pas davantage des « facultés » au « fond » de l'âme par les tâtonnements d'images approximatives. Il procède à l'inverse, partant de l'intuition de l'Unité pour aller à la découverte des choses en tant qu'elles sont ; ou encore, partant du centre de l'âme pour aboutir à l'acte, à la volonté, à la vie terrestre. En un mot : le mystique suit un chemin tout opposé à celui du poète ; son point de départ est la connaissance, non pas une interrogation lancée dans l'inconnu.

**

Ce schéma, auquel il faudrait apporter bien des nuances, nous permet peut-être de préciser dans quelle mesure l'assimilation de la poésie à la mystique est fallacieuse.

Il est une nécessité qu'il serait vain de

perdre de vue dans l'espoir de « spiritualiser » l'esthétique : nécessité de la *forme*, qui ne saurait, dans la poésie, être chose extérieure ou accessoire ; et c'est dire que le plan de la poésie, de l'art, ne coïncide jamais parfaitement avec celui de la mystique. Certes, il y a loin d'une conception formaliste, qui ne voit dans la métaphore autre chose que le produit d'une ingéniosité gratuite, à la poétique actuelle, qui y cherche le reflet d'une réalité transcendante ou l'instrument d'une sorcellerie divinatoire. Mais l'invention verbale peut être chargée de toute la dignité de connaissance que l'on voudra ; elle peut être assimilée à un acte titanesque de conquête irrationnelle, aussi maudit ou aussi sacré qu'il plaira de l'espérer : elle n'en demeure pas moins autre chose que l'acte mystique.

Il y a, en chacune de ces démarches, outre l'instant où elles se rapprochent, un surcroît, un « plus », qui est particulier à chacune d'elles. Faire confiance aux accidents de la pensée, aux révélations des mots assemblés, c'est affirmer qu'à travers le sensible quelque chose nous parle, autre chose, *mais qui demeure inconnu*. Ces révélations sont mystérieuses pour celui qui les obtient.

Celles du mystique sont pour lui lumineuses : il *sait*.

Le poète attend, s'abandonne à ce flot qui monte de lui-même, crée des formes dont il se persuade sans doute qu'elles ont un sens au delà d'elles-mêmes, mais sans savoir quel est ce sens : *il joue le jeu*.

Le mystique est le contraire même du joueur qui mise sur un chiffre dont il ignorerait la clef : il engage *son salut*, et connaître est, pour lui, synonyme d'être et de se sauver. L'« Union » peut être aussi brève que l'état privilégié qui est accordé au poète à de certains instants ; mais elle n'est limitée que si on la mesure selon notre temps : considérée dans son essence, elle est union avec Dieu, et par suite éternelle, intemporelle.

Quelle que soit la valeur que l'on attribue à l'acte poétique, il reste nécessairement un acte « médiat » (et non une union immédiate), un acte soumis à la nécessité de la forme, à des lois qui sont celles de la matière. Il aboutit à la parole, et, même convaincu que la parole n'a de sens que par allusion à la Nuit pressentie, le poète ne peut, sans cesser d'être poète, aller au delà de la parole. Le mystique tend au silence, et tout ce qui importe vraiment à ses yeux dépasse le verbe articulé.

Il ne s'agit pas, bien entendu, d'établir une hiérarchie entre la mystique et la poésie, si évident soit-il que, pour le mystique, la poésie, même spiritualisée dans les limites du possible, même dépouillée de ce qu'elle renferme peut-être nécessairement de révolte, demeure une activité inférieure par rapport à la voie de l'ascèse, de la contemplation et de l'union dans le silence. Celle-ci est, en langage théologique, une grâce, et à tout le moins un don qui n'appartient qu'à certains et tient à la structure de leur être. Elle ne peut être supérieure au sens absolu que pour celui qui en a reçu la faveur et fait l'expérience ; et nous ne jugeons pas de nos pouvoirs par rapport à ceux des anges.

Si la poésie la plus miraculeuse n'approche que de loin les régions de la certitude mystique, c'est aussi qu'elle a une autre fonction. Les chemins sont divers, par lesquels nous cherchons à rejoindre notre être le plus pur. A ceux qui sont destinés à entendre son message, la poésie apparaît revêtue d'une suprême dignité. Elle est l'expression de notre confiance et de notre orgueil, le réceptacle de notre angoisse personnelle aussi bien que de notre incorrigible espoir millénaire ; elle est quête d'un don mystérieux, d'une présence parfaite, et cette quête est peut-être défendue ou sans accomplissement possible. Mais elle est aussi concentration, dans toute la plénitude du mot, — le seul moyen que nous puissions entrevoir de donner l'harmonie à notre être entier, et de créer, du même coup, l'harmonie entre notre être et tout ce qui n'est pas lui. C'est là ce que nous nommons beauté et forme, qui n'est ni plus extérieur ni moins réellement un avertissement et une manifestation, que ce que nous appelons notre vie intérieure.

*
**

Ce problème des rapports entre la mystique et la poésie a été souvent obscurci par un emploi trop vague du mot « mystique » : faute de marquer les distinctions nécessaires entre la mystique et un mysticisme qui est le propre de l'âme primitive, on en vient facilement à assimiler le vœu de « magie », discernable dans la poésie actuelle, à une démarche mystique. Cette erreur a été commise, en particulier, à propos de Hugo, qui à certains moments eut un sentiment de la poésie si proche des modernes : ne se demandait-il pas, dès 1834, « jusqu'à quel point le chant appartient à la voix, et la poésie au poète » ? Et ne réclamait-il pas une langue « forgée pour tous les accidents possibles de la pensée » ?

Longtemps laissés dans l'ombre, les grands poèmes où Hugo a exprimé ses croyances religieuses ont toute la puissance et l'immédiateté des fables mythologiques. Et les thèmes essentiels de sa religion,

pananimisme, adhésion à certains faits en
dépit de toutes les contradictions logiques,
parenté entre l'homme et la nature « inférieure », identité de l'expression et de la
chose exprimée, sont exactement les thèmes
dominants de la psychologie « primitive ».
Considéré ainsi comme un extraordinaire
survivant des âges mythiques, comme un
esprit resté possesseur de pouvoirs que nous
avons échangés pour les dons de la culture
et les conquêtes intellectuelles, Hugo
reprend les proportions gigantesques que
l'autre siècle lui reconnaissait sur des titres
moins authentiques. Et c'est le très grand
mérite de M. Denis Saurat, que d'avoir,
dans sa *Religion de Victor Hugo* de 1929,
restitué sa véritable grandeur au poète.

Mais, lorsque M. Saurat, étudiant l'évolution spirituelle de Hugo, la compare aux
étapes parcourues sur la voie mystique
par les grands contemplatifs, il est beaucoup moins convaincant ; et il est obligé
d'invoquer l'existence probable de documents autobiographiques qui, publiés un
jour, devraient nous révéler cette vie intérieure de Hugo. La nature même de Hugo

rend peu vraisemblable l'existence de tels papiers intimes en dehors de son œuvre ; il y a chez lui une identité absolument indissociable entre la « vie intérieure » et l'expression poétique, imagée, et c'est à celle-ci qu'il faut s'en tenir pour toucher du doigt l'aventure singulière de Hugo, poète religieux.

Quant à rapprocher les étapes successives de la vie du poète, — l'alternance des angoisses et des euphories, les détresses totales et les triomphants cantiques des années 1850 à 1855, puis la sérénité active des dernières décades, — de la courbe de vie des grands mystiques, il y a là une assimilation qui paraît bien hâtive. Il ne suffit pas d'avoir désespéré sous le coup d'un deuil personnel et de reprendre confiance après avoir écouté les voix des tables tournantes, pour avoir connu la « nuit obscure » et l'union à Dieu. Nulle part, chez Hugo, nous ne trouvons ces deux voies conjuguées par lesquelles se définit la connaissance mystique : rien ne correspond chez lui à cette notion du « fond » de l'âme, de ce centre vers lequel il s'agit de descendre en dépassant le moi séparé ; — et rien, non plus, à cet anéantissement du « samsara », à cette succession destructive des apparences et des images qui se chassent pour laisser apparaître l'Unité seule existante. Que ce soit sur l'une ou l'autre de ces deux voies (approfondissement de soi ou contemplation de l'univers), la vie spirituelle de Hugo se passe, pour ainsi dire, *dans la région même des images.* Bien loin de remplir leur fonction mystique, celles-ci s'accumulent, dans une sorte d'ivresse au delà de laquelle Hugo ne saurait parvenir au sanctuaire de la contemplation sans images.

Le Dieu personnel de Hugo est une projection du moi du poète sur l'Infini, qui d'abord lui avait été Dieu. Comme le dit très justement M. Saurat : « Son intuition de sa propre personnalité était si développée qu'il portait en toute conception ce besoin de mettre des personnalités partout... Il sentait que Dieu était une personne, *comme lui, Hugo,* mais grandie à l'infini ».

Rien n'est plus différent de la mystique

que ce mysticisme : au lieu de l'absorption du moi en Dieu, absorption qui est anéantissement du moi séparé et qui se produit au terme de la plongée en soi, nous nous trouvons ici devant un élargissement infini du moi conquérant. Ce que l'on atteint sous la conduite de Hugo, ce n'est pas le Dieu *autre* des mystiques (ce Dieu dont l'existence leur interdit de dire que notre moi existe, car il est impossible que nous *soyons* de la même façon que Dieu) ; à quoi l'on aboutit, c'est à un Victor Hugo étendu, gonflé jusqu'aux limites de l'être, déifié tout entier. Le mouvement n'est point de concentration, mais d'expansion et de conquête.

Et l'expérience de Hugo sur l'autre voie, celle de la contemplation, se trouve définie du même coup ; elle est aux antipodes de la voie mystique. Ce n'est pas dans le « retour » d'une expérience « unitive » qu'il découvre la beauté du monde, et il ne commence pas par nier les apparences pour ne les retrouver, existantes, qu'en Dieu. Au contraire, Hugo cherche Dieu dans les choses, s'élève de la communication lyrique avec la nature à la pensée de Dieu. Là encore, le sentiment premier de Hugo n'a rien de commun avec celui du mystique, qui sait *d'abord* que l'Unité seule existe. Chez Hugo, la conscience inébranlable du moi individuel s'accompagne de la confrontation de ce moi avec l'immensité, l'infini, l'abîme des espaces. Cette confrontation, d'abord effrayée et tremblante, ne deviendra ivresse que dans l'instant où le poète visionnaire aura absorbé en lui l'immensité et étendu ses propres limites jusqu'à se confondre avec l'univers.

Certes, on peut à juste titre parler du « mysticisme » de Hugo, mais au sens particulier et très élargi où M. Seillère entend ce terme : au sens d'un « impérialisme du moi », qui est la chose la plus contraire à la mystique véritable. C'est en effet méconnaître profondément l'essence de celle-ci que de l'assimiler, comme on ne le fait que trop souvent, à un geste, ou même à une simple sensation d'expansion.

On pourrait dire que Hugo ne procède

jamais d'une intuition à son expression, mais toujours du spectacle au spectacle, et qu'ainsi sa vie « intérieure » n'échappe jamais au plan de la vision ; ou encore, en paraphrasant un mot de Paul Valéry, que « ce qu'il y a de plus intérieur en lui, c'est l'œil ». D'un bout à l'autre de sa longue fécondité, on est frappé par la permanence des mêmes images et des mêmes gestes, qui, d'abord purement extérieurs, spectaculaires ou physiques, reçoivent simplement avec les années une valeur symbolique et s'inscrivent dans un mythe étonnamment cohérent. L'ombre et la lumière, qui ne font encore, dans la jeunesse du poète, que jeter leurs contrastes sur le monde terrestre, finissent, dans l'admirable poème de la *Fin de Satan*, par traduire l'opposition du Bien et du Mal : et en réalité, il y a là plus qu'une « traduction » ; l'image se confond avec ce qu'elle signifie et s'y amalgame si bien qu'il est impossible de dégager une « idée » hugolienne du Bien et du Mal, qui serait dépouillée de cette perception imagée.

Il est vrai qu'un texte des brouillons de

Dieu peut, au premier regard, sembler décrire une « mort du moi » très voisine des expériences mystiques :

> *Dans l'obscurité sourde, impalpable, inouïe,*
> *Je me retrouvai seul, mais je n'étais plus moi ;*
> *Ou du moins, dans ma tête ouverte aux vents d'effroi,*
> *Je sentis, sans pourtant que l'ombre et le mystère*
> *Eussent cassé le fil qui me lie à la terre,*
> *Monter, grossir, entrer presque au dernier repli,*
> *Comme une crue étrange et terrible d'oubli ;*
> *Je sentis, dans la forme obscure pour moi-même*
> *Que je suis et qui, brume, erre dans le problème,*
> *Presque s'évanouir tout l'être antérieur...*
> *...A peine de ma vie avais-je encore l'idée,*
> *Et ce que jusqu'alors, larve aux lueurs guidée,*
> *J'avais nommé mon âme était je ne sais quoi*
> *Dont je n'étais plus sûr et qui flottait en moi.*
> *Il ne restait de moi qu'une soif de connaître,*
> *Une aspiration vers ce qui pourrait être,*
> *Une bouche voulant boire un peu d'eau qui fuit,*
> *Fût-ce au creux de la main fatale de la nuit.*

On sent assez, pourtant, que ce « vaste oubli » n'a nullement le sens que les mystiques donnent au *vivo ego, jam non ego* de saint Paul ; si l'être extérieur et la mémoire de l'existence séparée s'effacent dans les deux expériences, c'est par une tendance et un mouvement tout inverse. Chez le mystique, la conscience du moi fait place à une *vie* plus intense : *sed Christus vivit in me*. Le moi s'est résorbé dans une *concentration*, au terme de laquelle il reste une plénitude, une conscience accrue : celle d'une « présence », d'une union ineffable. Chez Hugo, c'est tout le contraire, une diminution de la sensation d'être, une rupture des barrières *vers l'extérieur*, une dissolution dans je ne sais quoi de flottant. Plus rien ne se nomme l'âme, ne correspond à cette réalité touchée concrètement par le mystique au cœur de l'extase. Au lieu d'une certitude, il n'est demeuré qu'une « soif de connaître », cette connaissance fût-elle maudite et nocturne !

La mystique n'est pas ivresse, mais progrès, et cheminement vers une lumière *certaine ;* elle ne saurait être cette jouissance formidable et sensuelle qu'atteint Hugo dans ses essors éperdus à travers les espaces indéterminés et les gouffres habités par les larves, ce spectacle prodigieux que se donne un moi glouton.

Hugo est un grand primitif parce qu'il est un grand créateur de mythes et d'images ; l'image en elle-même est à jamais inséparable, chez lui, de la réalité qu'elle exprime. Et peut-être l'extraordinaire phénomène que représente ce primitif en plein âge de culture est-il bien fait pour nous rappeler que poésie et magie, ensorcellement musical et sorcellerie proprement dite sont étroitement apparentés.

Mais précisément, par rapport à la magie, la mystique constitue un pas vers la conscience ; le mystique ne peut accomplir son expérience que si justement il « s'arrache » à tout ce qui fait l'essence même de la sorcellerie primitive ou de la magie poétique : s'il renonce à cette région qui est celle des mythes aussi bien que des créations poétiques : à cette région où expression et chose exprimée sont identiques. Et ainsi, dès que l'on reconnaît dans la poésie une tentative pour recouvrer ces pouvoirs magiques dont l'humanité fut douée en ses premiers âges, — et la poésie moderne est pour une bonne part cette tentative, — on reconnaît la différence de nature entre poésie et mystique. Vie mystique et « primitivisme » sont à jamais inconciliables.

NOTES

Les deux essais que je réunis ici ont été écrits indépendamment l'un de l'autre. On voudra bien, peut-être, y discerner des préoccupations semblables, qui justifient leur réunion.

*
* *

L'étude sur *Aurélia*, ébauchée voici plusieurs années, doit beaucoup à la documentation que M. Aristide Marie a publiée dans sa grande biographie. Et je tiens à reconnaître que M. Henri Clouard, dans son livre sur Nerval comme dans les préfaces de son édition, a su voir souvent toute l'envergure du drame spirituel qui se joue dans *Aurélia*.

Je n'ignore pas les interprétations que l'on a données, à diverses reprises, des sonnets des *Chimères*, soit en remontant aux sources littéraires de ces poèmes comme le fait M. F. Constans, dans la *Revue de Littérature comparée* de 1934, soit en recourant à la tradition occulte, comme M. Rolland de Renéville dans un récent article des *Nouvelles Littéraires*. Ces diverses exégèses sont précieuses ; mais il ne me semble pas qu'aucune d'elles soit absolument convaincante, ni surtout qu'elles « expliquent » vraiment ce qui restera toujours inexplicable dans les sonnets de Nerval.

* ***

On aura reconnu tout ce que mes définitions de la poésie moderne doivent au beau livre de M. Raymond : *De Baudelaire au Surréalisme* (Corrêa, 1933), dont il est impossible de se passer aujourd'hui lorsqu'on se préoccupe de poésie.

Quant à l'expérience mystique, je dois beaucoup à l'admirable *Saint-Jean-de-la-Croix* de M. J. Baruzi (1931), — au livre de M. R. Otto : *West-Oestliche Mystik* (1926) et à celui de Mrs. E. Underhill : *Die Mystik*.

Le problème des rapports entre les deux expériences a été étudié maintes fois depuis que l'abbé Bremond l'a soulevé. L'excellente revue belge *Hermès* a apporté, depuis 1934, d'importantes contributions à cette étude. Tout récemment, M. Rolland de Renéville a donné, dans *Mesures*, une excellente analyse de ce problème. Je n'ai pas cru devoir changer, après l'avoir lue, le plan de ces notes, qui étaient écrites dans leurs grandes lignes (et publiées en partie dans la revue *Présence*) dès mars 1934. Il m'a paru préférable de les laisser subsister telles qu'elles sont, sans y ajouter certains compléments que j'aurais pu emprunter à M. Rolland de Renéville : nous partons de définitions assez différentes, et nos conclusions mêmes sont assez peu identiques, pour que certains résultats semblables, obtenus par des voies diverses, aient leur intérêt. M. Rolland de Renéville s'est appliqué à suivre de plus près que moi les phases parallèles des deux expériences, et il a appuyé son analyse de citations bien précieuses. Je crois cependant qu'il ne marque pas assez un élément essentiel de la mystique, qui est la volonté de *salut*.

*
* *

J'ai tenté ailleurs (*Revue de Littérature comparée*, 1934) de suivre à travers l'œuvre de Hugo les mille formes successives d'une image : celle de l'orbite vide, au fond des cieux, signifiant l'absence de Dieu. Peut-être empruntée au fameux Songe de Jean-Paul, retrouvée sans doute dans le *Christ aux Oliviers* de Nerval, cette image n'a cessé de se transformer et de reparaître dans l'œuvre de Hugo. Il faudrait multiplier ces études de détail, pour démontrer clairement que Hugo vit sur le plan des images, et pour percer un peu de ce mystère qui enveloppe encore son œuvre.

*
* *

Le jour même où j'envoie mon manuscrit à l'imprimerie, je lis dans *Mesures* un admirable essai de M. G. Bounoure : *Abîmes de V. Hugo*, qui évoque les paysages intérieurs du poète avec la même profondeur qui distingue toutes les pages de ce rare commentateur de la poésie.

Et la *Nouvelle Revue Française* de novembre 1936 apporte un nouvel essai de M. de Renéville, l'un des meilleurs qu'il ait publiés, sur *Le Sens de la Nuit :* outre une parfaite analyse des Hymnes de Novalis, on y trouvera sur Nerval des pages bien remarquables.

UNE LETTRE INÉDITE
DE GÉRARD DE NERVAL.

Un collectionneur parisien a bien voulu me permettre de prendre copie du billet autographe suivant, adressé à *Monsieur, Monsieur Louis Ulbach, 25, rue de Monceau* :

Mon cher Monsieur,

Décidément je crois qu'il vaut mieux attendre et ne pas donner tout de suite à composer. Du reste je n'en ai pas pour longtemps et nous verrons mieux cela la semaine prochaine. La coupure en deux morceaux aurait peut-être des inconvéniens, vu du reste le peu de longueur qui pourrait nuire à l'un ou à l'autre des morceaux.

Pardon de ces hésitations, mais le genre difficile du travail me rend timide pour la forme de publication.

Votre bien dévoué,

Gérard DE NERVAL.

La feuille à en-tête de la *Librairie nouvelle,
15, Boulevard des Italiens, en face de la Maison
dorée, Jacottet et Bourdilliat, éditeurs*, n'est pas
datée, mais porte, imprimés, les mots : *Paris,
le ... 185 .* — J'ai cru d'abord que ce billet,
postérieur à 1850, pouvait se rapporter à *Aurélia :* il prouverait alors que l'œuvre était bien
achevée aux yeux de son auteur, malgré les
affirmations contraires de ses amis qui l'édi-
tèrent. Mais si « le genre difficile du travail »
peut, en effet, désigner *Aurélia*, « le peu de
longueur » étonne. Parmi les œuvres publiées
en revue après 1850, seuls l'essai sur *Quintus
Aucler* (en entier dans la *Revue de Paris*, nov.
1851), et la fulgurante nouvelle *Pandora* (la
première partie seule parut, dans le *Mousque-
taire* du 31 oct. 1854 ; la seconde, retrouvée en
épreuves, fut publiée en 1921 seulement par
M. A. Marie) pourraient entrer en ligne de
compte. Les hésitations de Gérard à propos
de cette nouvelle, qu'il retira à la dernière
minute du recueil des *Filles du Feu*, peuvent
faire croire que ce billet s'y rapporte. Mais
l'eût-il appelée un « travail » ?

TABLE

Gérard de Nerval et la descente
aux enfers   9

Poésie et mystique. 97

Notes 137

Lettre inédite de Nerval . . . 143

CE LIVRE

EST SORTI DES PRESSES

DE L'IMPRIMERIE DARANTIERE

A DIJON

EN DÉCEMBRE

M.CM.XXXVI

Herbert W. [illegible]

Review for [illegible] management

LIVING ISSUES
IN RELIGION

Edited by
Miles H. Krumbine, D.D.

OTHER BOOKS BY
SHAILER MATHEWS

SELECT MEDIAEVAL DOCUMENTS
THE FRENCH REVOLUTION, 1789-1815
NEW TESTAMENT TIMES IN PALESTINE
THE SPIRITUAL INTERPRETATION OF HISTORY

PATRIOTISM AND RELIGION
THE MAKING OF TOMORROW
THE VALIDITY OF AMERICAN IDEALS

JESUS ON SOCIAL INSTITUTIONS
THE SOCIAL GOSPEL
THE INDIVIDUAL AND THE SOCIAL GOSPEL
THE CHURCH AND THE CHANGING ORDER

THE GOSPEL AND THE MODERN MAN
THE FAITH OF MODERNISM
THE MESSIANIC HOPE IN THE NEW TESTAMENT
THE ATONEMENT AND THE SOCIAL PROCESS
CONTRIBUTIONS OF SCIENCE TO RELIGION
(WITH 13 SCIENTISTS)
A CONSTRUCTIVE LIFE OF CHRIST
(WITH E. D. BURTON)
A DICTIONARY OF RELIGION AND ETHICS
(WITH G. B. SMITH)
THE STUDENT'S GOSPELS
(WITH E. J. GOODSPEED)
IMMORTALITY AND THE COSMIC PROCESS
THE GROWTH OF THE IDEA OF GOD

CHRISTIANITY
AND
SOCIAL PROCESS

*BARROWS LECTURES
FOR 1933-1934*

BY
SHAILER MATHEWS

PUBLISHERS
HARPER & BROTHERS
NEW YORK AND LONDON
1934

CHRISTIANITY AND SOCIAL PROCESS

Copyright, 1934, by Harper & Brothers
Printed in the United States of America

All rights in this book are reserved.
No part of the text may be reproduced in any
manner whatsoever without written permis-
sion. For information address
Harper & Brothers

FIRST EDITION

K–I

TABLE OF CONTENTS

I
RELIGION AND SOCIAL BEHAVIOR
page 1

II
CHRISTIANITY AS AN ASPECT OF WESTERN CIVILIZATION
page 33

III
THE MORAL NATURE OF THE CHRISTIAN RELIGION
page 57

IV
CHRISTIANITY AND THE INDIVIDUAL
page 98

V
CHRISTIANITY AND THE MORALITY OF GROUPS
page 129

VI
CHRISTIANITY AND ECONOMICS
page 150

VII
CHRISTIANITY AND INTERNATIONALISM
page 179

PREFACE

This volume is composed of the Barrows Lectures of the University of Chicago, for 1933-34. They are somewhat expanded from those actually delivered, but retain the point of view and purpose which the Foundation demands. These, in the words of Mrs. Caroline E. Haskell's title of gift are to present "to the scholarly and thoughtful people of India" "in a friendly, temperate and conciliatory way and in the fraternal spirit which pervaded the Parliament of Religions, the great questions of the truths of Christianity, its harmonies with the truths of other religions, its rightful claims and the best methods of setting them forth." Such liberal formulas warrant an objective historical approach to the place of Christianity in social life and the treatment adopted is that of the historian rather than the apologist. So far as I can see the religious problems of India

Preface

are akin to those of the West, and I trust that Indian scholars may study the social aspects of their religions in the same spirit and method with which I have endeavored to trace the relations of Christianity and Western civilization.

SHAILER MATHEWS

CHRISTIANITY
AND
SOCIAL PROCESS

I

RELIGION AND SOCIAL BEHAVIOR

To understand the relations of Christianity and society one must be historically minded. Such an attitude of mind is seldom possessed by either the theologian or the social reformer. To the former Christianity is a series of debatable truths derived from an infallible Scripture, and to the latter Jesus is a lay figure upon which to hang social programs. It is not strange, therefore, that what should be a historical and sociological study has been distorted into a defense or a criticism. The champions of Christianity declare—to use the title of a ponderous mid-Victorian volume—that its divine origin has been indicated by its historical results, and every improvement in human relations has been identified with these results. On the other hand, the critics of Christianity picture it as deadening discontent with earthly ills by the opiate of the hope of heaven. Even those who would claim scientific method are apt to see Christianity through the atmosphere of primitive religions. Such indifference to historical facts has been repeatedly rationalized as a philosophy. Christianity has been treated as a system of truths interpreted as if there were neither time nor space, historical relativity nor social process, human beings nor religious institutions, but only true or false formulas. The ease of organizing such formulas varies as they are removed from observable human experience. It is no more difficult to talk about an unknown God who has been revealed apart from human history in His Word, than it has been to argue about decrees issued by God before there was any universe and to describe a heaven which lies beyond the stars. It is little wonder that men in moments of distress should prefer formulas incapable of verification as an escape technique from social tasks. They turn from a God whom they cannot find in the processes of history to a God who will triumph by flood, fire, or cosmic destruction.

Religion and Social Behavior

There are many causes for this retreat toward monasticism and mysticism, dogmatism and liberalism, but they all are rooted in a failure to recognize that Christianity is not a series of abstract truths, but a religion. If we are to discover what is its relationship to our own day we should know what has been its relationship to social process in the past. To discover this demands the methods of the historian and the sociologist. The philosopher, the theologian, the apologete, and the humanist should not be indifferent to the findings of a socio-historical method. Nothing is to be gained by reliance upon epigrams. Even though Christians may have been stupid and hypocritical, the Christian religion has been an element of Western civilization.

Now a religion is a form of social behavior resulting from the interplay of many forces. Chief among these is the extension of the biological urge to gain proper adjustment with an environment which so often seems dominated by chance. Men have felt themselves dependent upon the forces of nature and have sought to gain help from them by treating them as they treat one another; that is to say, personally. All religions have the same function, but their techniques vary according to the culture and social practices of their adherents. Christianity is no exception to this rule. Like every other religion, it is a form of social behavior. In it, as in other religions, men have developed beliefs, customs, institutions, organizations, intended to facilitate the gaining of help from the supernatural. To discuss the truth of various religions regardless of their social origins and relations is to plunge into abstractions and drift toward metaphysics. For the historically-minded person the primary interest is that of discovering just what a religion is. The first result of such an effort is the conviction that a religion is an aspect of a social order, and that its significance can be judged by the customs and institutions it has organized, the economic and political influence it has exerted, the social classes and domestic groups it has maintained, the sanctions it gives to morals, and the power it has to stimulate or to check social change. In such an estimate there will be, of course, a recognition of the function of a religion to console and cheer the individual, but its capacity in this

Religion and Social Behavior

regard will be seen to be inseparable from the influence of the customs and beliefs which are embodied in the total group life of its followers. Every religion is seen to be a specific type of social behavior, with socialized customs and beliefs conditioning the experiences of individuals who constitute the religious group. It both appropriates and affects the economic and political elements of a social order as they emerge from a social process.

To judge a mature religion as if it were a vestige of primitivity argues a limited knowledge of social behavior and institutions. It is as unscientific as it would be to belittle chemistry because chemists once explained fire by phlogiston, or radioactivity because alchemists believed in the philosopher's stone.

I

A social order is not a mere aggregate of institutions. It is the outcome of a complicated social process. Geography and climate, industry and politics, education and social customs, are in its pedigree. The past persists in the present and, more or less transformed, reaches into the future. In some social orders it becomes tyrannical, forbidding further change; in others it is easily modified. But there is no break in history. Even periods of revolution cannot escape the influences of the past. Institutions have grown out of institutions, customs out of customs, social habits and classes have changed as economic conditions have altered. By a sort of trial-and-error method customs which have been found to be advantageous have been preserved; others which have been found to be injurious have been modified or abandoned. In some civilizations this evolutionary process has moved more rapidly than in others, but even where it has been checked it has existed.

A social process is not an abstract concept. Historians cannot venture to speak of "the" social process of unhistorical thinkers. They are concerned with definite streams of human activities and change which are as concrete as humanity itself. It is people who reorganize their inherited customs and institutions, who change habits and desires, who adopt new methods for satisfying their felt needs. Such a process is not necessarily progress. The institutions and customs of one age

Religion and Social Behavior

may be replaced by those of lesser value, or even destroyed without successors. There have been periods in which catastrophe or decay has overtaken a civilization. In speaking of process we do not pass judgment on social change; we simply recognize the fact that human history is genetic. Radical changes it has known, but even these were subject to the laws of continuity. Whether or not such laws, as has been claimed by some, include cycles of change in which a civilization is born, develops, and dies, the process is undeniable. Until the genetic relations of the elements of a culture and a civilization are recognized, history becomes unintelligible.

Every religion is an aspect of a social process. The convictions, hopes, fears, customs, institutions which result from the attempt to satisfy the needs of a social group by appeal to the superhuman are transmitted from generation to generation. These techniques have much in common. Their function is the same. They are all means of setting up personal relations with those superhuman activities upon which men believe themselves dependent.

Christianity and Social Process

Such use of social experience varies with social practices. Religions differ as societies differ.

This use of social experience is, however, not the only technique by which men have attempted to set up help-gaining relations with or to control nature. In the more primitive societies there has been magic, and as knowledge has developed there has been science—in both of which impersonal relations are recognized. But even they have not been altogether free from habits of mind derived from social experience. In primitive cultures there is no sharp distinction between these two methods of compelling nature to satisfy human needs. In agriculture men performed the manual labor to obtain their crops, but they also established fasts, feasts, dances, sacrifices, which were intended to placate whatever supernatural forces or persons they supposed controlled agricultural processes. There developed, in consequence, correct ways of behavior. Certain persons were believed to have peculiar ability to propose various acts which would establish helpful relations with these supernatural powers. There were feasts to which the supernatural persons could be invited;

there were prayers with which favor could be gained; there were teachings, often esoteric, preserved and transmitted as laws. Most important of all, there were ways of living which were approved by the deities of the respective groups. These deities were not necessarily feared, but they were apt to be jealous of their prerogatives. Men offered sacrifices, observed sacred rites, regulated their habits and their food, prayed, supported priests, established feast days and fast days, because they thought by so doing they could gain help in satisfying their needs, avoiding danger and gaining happiness after death. Men have sought superhuman assistance because of their own impotence. Nature abounds in tragedies. Sickness and death, misfortunes of many sorts, social disorders and natural catastrophes, have always marked the history of humanity. In all crises men have instinctively sought help from sources greater than their own skill. Such behavior cannot universally be traced to fear of chance or the dead. Men have not always thought of such aid as coming from personal deities, and they have not always rational-

Christianity and Social Process

ized their search for aid, but in moments of need, when crops fail and poverty increases, when the tension of human relations grows unendurable, when loved ones are lost and causes fail, when misinterpretation ruins friendships and wrongdoing brings remorse, when plans must be made for future action in peace or war, men have sought aid from sources which are more than human. The methods of such search which have been judged to be effective have grown into group customs. Thus a religion has been born.

But religions, it must be remembered, are more than their primitive origins. As a culture has developed men have rationalized this social behavior. In many cases the tension between it and intellectual achievements has been severe. Then it is that men have abandoned practices which no longer seemed in accordance with reality and have undertaken to discover new ways of satisfying their needs. The area of a religion has then grown circumscribed. Scientific techniques have replaced religious practices. The influence of the religious group upon other groups resulting from a social process grows indirect. Yet it is none the less present, for it is itself one aspect of that process.

II

Every great civilization has produced a religion. In some cases, as in Judaism, it has remained the property of a race, or as in Hinduism, of both a race and a locality. Other religions, like Mohammedanism and Buddhism and Christianity, have spread into many social orders and have been affected by the processes which characterized such orders. In consequence new groups have been developed. Each of them has preserved distinguishing characteristics of its origins, but each has embodied beliefs, habits of thought and behavior derived from the culture within which it has developed.

Religious sanction came to be attached to certain acts rather than to others because they involved man's dependence upon his deities. Often a deity is described as dictating or even writing laws for his people. What the deity commanded was believed to be for the good of the tribe or the nation. Prosperity was expected to follow obedience to divine directions as to behavior, and calamity was punishment for disobedience. Sometimes this punishment was in the form of calamities like earthquakes and storms, famine and fire, disease and death; sometimes it was personal distress, national, political, or military defeat. It was natural, therefore, to believe that prosperity argued divine favor because of man's obedience, while misfortune argued the contrary. In one of the so-called Psalms of Solomon, written not long after the capture of Jerusalem by Pompey, there is a striking illustration of this religious interpretation of national misfortune. The author thus represents his nation lamenting its collapse:

> Certainly the alarm of war was here before me;
> I said, "God will hearken unto me for I am full of righteousness."
> I considered in my heart that I was full of righteousness because I was prosperous and had become plenteous in children.
> Their [the Maccabean rulers] riches were gone forth unto all the world and their glory unto the ends of the earth.

Religion and Social Behavior

> They were lifted up to the stars; they said,
> "We shall never fall."
> But they waxed haughty in their prosperity
> and were not able to endure.
> Their sins were in secret and I knew it not.

Such distress of mind is understandable. A deity indifferent to the disloyalty of his followers can hardly expect to maintain their respect. The most significant thing for our purpose, however, is that these commands of the god upon obedience to which the prosperity of the individual or of the people depend, involve social practices as well as cultural requirements. They determine the morals which a group conserves. The gods may be displeased or pleased by any behavior. In the Hebrew Pentateuch, the Laws of Manu, and the Upanishads, the deity sets forth the directions as to nearly every relation of life. The ancient Roman religion was largely a collection of social practices and some god or goddess was believed to be concerned with every detail of life. As the Jewish faith developed through generations of rabbis, the very minutiæ of life found themselves included in the divine legislation. Indeed, religion among great masses of people may almost be said to be the maintenance of proper customs in all the elemental activities of life. Birth, puberty, marriage, death have their appropriate recognition as a condition of prosperity. The planting and the harvesting of crops, the maintenance of herds and flocks, the building of bridges and buildings, associations with other persons, the preparation for battle, not to mention innumerable other matters, are all given religious significance. The favor of the gods is conditioned upon the proper performance of customs which, constituting a social heritage from a distant past, are traced back to divine establishment and regarded as explicit commands of supernatural beings. The effort to gain merit which shall assure good fortune after death has led to acts of social significance.

III

These facts forbid approaching a religion from the side of philosophy alone. Religion and philosophy have been closely associated, but no religion can be fully understood merely by a study of its literature. The anthropologists have ac-

Religion and Social Behavior

quainted us with religions which have no sacred literature. A religion possesses social control through prescribed social customs far more than through its philosophy. The conception of religion as a search for truth must be supplemented by a conception of religions as forms of social behavior affecting other behaviors of a culture.

The intellectual element of each religion is varied and, roughly speaking, expressive of the cultural life of its followers. It may in time take form in a philosophy, as in Hinduism, or in a theology, as in Christianity, but it is always an aspect of a social order, the practices and customs of which it uses as patterns of thought. Men have treated their gods as they treat their fellow men, and attribute to them characteristics which mark social superiors. In the case of the major religions, their literary and philosophical formulations represent the noblest aspects of a civilization. As Epictetus exclaimed long ago, "Do not all the philosophers talk about God?" True, within any large social group holding a religion, there is a vast spread between the intellectual attitudes of persons representing social extremes. Great masses

Christianity and Social Process

of people have no interest in theology or in philosophy. Their religion consists in observing the various practices and customs and other forms of behavior which have been regarded as enabling men to avoid misfortune and to get help from the gods or god they worship. More intellectual persons have abandoned many of the practices, although some, indeed many, of these, have persisted as conventions like the modern respect for Santa Claus and fairies. There will occasionally appear persons and small groups so sophisticated as to abandon completely any form of religious behavior. Yet even in their case the abandonment is not so complete as they would have it appear. Customs sanctioned by religious authority have become embodied in a social order and are still operative. So important is this loyalty to the group and its practices that some scholars have seen it as actually constituting religion, the group unity being symbolized by some totem and thus becoming the god of the tribe. Even if such an hypothesis can hardly account for the rise of a religion, it is correct in so far as it recognizes that a religion is an organization of group practices and that those

Religion and Social Behavior

practices have a meaning and purpose which belong in the realm of values. This is now generally recognized by those who deal with the philosophy of a religion, and many definitions of religion as a general term center around the preservation of social values. Each religion is a social behavior preserving and expressing—sometimes very imperfectly—what are believed to be permanent values.

IV

From the attempts to extend personal relations and social practices to relations with the superhuman powers, have developed concepts of God and the religious sanctions of morality. Personal adjustment implies personal response. Men have used whatever conception seemed to them final in their social experience as a means of setting forth reciprocal relations with some higher power. In the West the conception of God has followed the development of the evolving civilization. Naturally, in a pre-scientific age, the pattern used was that of politics, and men thought of God as an absolute sovereign. Much of the theological think-

Christianity and Social Process

ing of Christianity was shaped in corollaries of this conception, and theology became transcendentalized politics. But the actual religious life of the West is not to be identified with its theological formulas. While its learned men have been endeavoring to think of the God substance as tripersonal and to justify prayer, faith, and the hope for life beyond death, the people themselves have been praying, performing such rites and following such practices as they believed would assure good fortune on earth and blessed immortality in heaven. Theology has had its part in clarifying the thought of God, justifying beliefs and organizing the duties incident to the religious life. As variations in experience and inheritance have grown more pronounced, a group has tended to seek new formulas in which to give intellectual support and system to religious behavior. Persons whose dominant attitude is scientific are using such scientific patterns as the relation of the organism to its environment. Just as the subjects of an absolute sovereign used the politics of their day to express the relation of men and God, so democrats are endeavoring to use the symbols of

Religion and Social Behavior

democracy. Scientists have increasingly concerned themselves with the impersonal environment, and modern Christians have found in the development of personal values their most effective goal for conduct.

Difficulties regarding moral behavior naturally arise from changes in patterns of the idea of God. We easily identify the form of our thought with its content, and use the one as well as the other as a major premise from which to draw specific conclusions. Practices and ideals that are the extension of a religious pattern become sacred. The habit, for example, of pleading liturgically with God for mercy is the outcome of the conception of him as a supreme unconstitutional ruler of the sort known to those who originated the liturgy. So, too, the need of substitutionary suffering, intended to satisfy the dignity or punitive justice of God, is derived from social practices. Originally springing from a useful analogy, these portrayals of the divine character have been treated as literal facts. To realize them as anything less is to cause confusion in many earnest minds. They fear lest in

Christianity and Social Process

abandoning inherited ideas of God men may lose their sense of right and wrong.

The effect upon Christian beliefs of the new understanding of nature, which arose in the West during the latter part of the nineteenth century and the first quarter of the present century was often destructive. Men's imaginations were appalled by the vastness of the material universe, and it was considered the proper thing to speak of men as cogs in a great machine. In place of religion there was the elevation of the will to power, or the philosophy of futility and frustration. Such anti-religious forces were greatly stimulated by the World War. Confronted with the operations of national and economic interests which seemed beyond the control of individuals, men turned to coerced programs as their sole means of escape from the effect of a mechanistic universe and a depersonalized social order.

All religions are today passing through the same experience. Customs, morals, institutions which have been given divine sanction and have been passed from each generation to its successor are, so to speak, being subjected to a new social

Religion and Social Behavior

climate. Those influences which we roughly call modernity are so changing the conditions under which men live and are introducing so many impersonal conceptions of man's relationship to the universe as to change modes of religious thought. Most of these changes are the immediate effects of physical and biological sciences which have substituted the ideas of impersonal force for the acts of deities. Instead of praying, men experiment, and after having discovered the *modus operandi* of natural forces they make machines to do what the gods were once asked to do.

V

It is impossible to separate a religion from morality. They are aspects of the same social behavior. Meditation may seem very distant from almsgiving or marriage ceremonies, but even the man who retires from the world to pass his time in meditation is in so doing passing judgment upon practices which he believes hinder him in the development of his own personal life. Furthermore, he is himself reckoning upon the continuance of social practices on the part of others as a means

Christianity and Social Process

by which to gain his support. A social order that did not minister to the needs of those who make no economic contribution to its welfare would soon put an end to such non-economic living.

Morals and religion are aspects of the same social process. Modifications within that process may disclose new needs of divine help. When a people, for instance, passes from a cold climate to a hot climate where there is need of rain rather than of sun, not only are the pictures and powers of the deity changed, but the customs acceptable to the deity and so calculated to further the welfare of a group are changed. When a tribe that has been nomadic becomes agricultural, supernatural help is needed for the raising of crops and the maintenance of proper climatic conditions rather than the maintenance of flocks and herds. New customs at the same time are developed and new *mores* unsuited to nomadic life are given sanction by divine will. One has only to watch the development of the Hebrew law as it is reflected in the Old Testament to see how morality and religion are really aspects of the same effort to organize life for the maintenance of social goods.

Religion and Social Behavior

Changes within a religion may also come from the interpenetration of cultures and civilizations. A people that has been completely circumscribed and has excluded all foreign influences may find the walls of its exclusiveness being broken down. The old authorities seem incapable of meeting the new needs which result from such readjustment. When the introduction of machinery leads to an abandonment of the productive processes of a people, the distribution of population, and the development of a capitalist social order, the consequent tension affects more than conventions. A new set of needs is developed which the old customs authorized by social inheritance and sanctioned by religion are incapable of satisfying. A change which comes under such conditions is oftentimes tragic and the moral attitude resulting is often that of bewilderment. I remember a conversation with Viscount Shibusawa in Japan, a man of singular distinction and intellectual penetration. He said that years before, when the Western practices were first coming into Japan, somebody asked him whether he thought that Japanese life could maintain itself in the midst of such new forces. He had replied, he said, that

Christianity and Social Process

he thought the Japanese spirit would be able to accomplish that end. But, he said with deep feeling, "I was mistaken." He then went on to say how he had attempted, by establishing the Society of Concordia, to discover in the various religions some common elements which would control and give direction to the change through which the Japanese nation was passing. Such a search is being made by followers of many religions who sense the impotence of religious beliefs and practices derived from ancient cultures to direct social behavior in modern conditions.

Revolutionary changes in intellectual attitudes may well give serious concern to one who sees in religion a conservative and inspiring element of a social order. The abandonment of any element of social control, however justified it may be, carries with it consequences other than itself. The disintegration of authority at any point in social life is apt to induce wide changes in behavior. To a considerable extent conventional morality, as we have seen, has grown up around a definite conception as to the relation of God to human conduct as that of a lawgiver. When fear of God dis-

Religion and Social Behavior

appears, distrust is sure to arise relative to the morality organized by a group in accordance with his laws. I would not be understood as indicating that every man who gives up the idea of a divine sovereign runs amuck through the Ten Commandments. Such a view is counter to experience and to good sense. But no one can come in contact with lives that have not yet reached self-direction, without viewing with apprehension any breakdown in idealistic control or the abandonment, without the substitution of new beliefs, of what is regarded as an intellectually untenable faith. It is not so much that men and women deliberately undertake to be moral anarchs, as that the disintegrating process proceeds unobserved through the entire structure of their inner life. Cynical views as to justice and honesty and chastity are easy for minds who no longer fear the punishments once dreaded at the hands of a heavenly King. The perspective of values becomes disarranged. Lives grow morally soft because they lack religious censorship. The abandonment of religious conventions has within it the possibilities of moral tragedy. Particularly is this true of those who accept the destruction of

Christianity and Social Process

inherited religious formulas without intelligently realizing the constructive elements that lie when scientific thought is applied to religion. Both men and women have too often felt that they were free to act in accordance with any impulse. Social behavior is bewildered. The permanence of the family as a social institution is already threatened. Questions of sex are being given new answers with the rise of birth control and the emergence of economic conditions which make marriage of comparatively young persons economically difficult. Women, after as well as before marriage, are claiming new privileges because of economic independence. Laws derived from the older social structure are not enforced and very often are ignored.

Obviously such a situation is headed toward social disintegration and disorder unless it can be controlled by ideals which are farther reaching than those inherited from a less complicated social order. The situation will never be clarified by merely making new laws, although good people easily yield to the temptation to make civil authority enforce their ideals. Where, however, be-

Religion and Social Behavior

cause of religious uncertainty, ethical ideals no longer possess the power of self-enforcement, the morale of a social order is threatened.

VI

Such facts as these make it plain that the relation of a religion to any social process is to be discovered in human lives quite as much as in teachings organized in sacred literatures. For a religion is the behavior of a group that is carrying forward certain ideals and perpetuating certain customs and institutions within a social process. It is by no means certain to respond to that process. There is in a religious group an *esprit de corps* which often makes toward a fanatical group loyalty. Its own interest gets sanction from its fear of or loyalty to supernatural activities. It is inevitable that a religious movement should grow conservative as it becomes organized. It fears to change customs and practices believed to be approved by the Deity. The religious innovator in any social order is suspected if not hated. Like Uzzah he is touching sacred things and is liable to bring the displeasure of the Deity not only upon himself but upon the group which has permitted such action. Prophets, reformers, and heretics are judged enemies of society in that they seek to change that which the Deity has approved and upon which the prosperity of the community depends. With such a psychology it is not strange that religious organizations have initiated few if any social reforms, that they have been champions of the *status quo*. Their gods are not interested in social change; the oppressed and unfortunate must look for justice in the future life.

But a religion that has become socially immobile is likely to produce individuals or minority groups who seek its readjustment to unsatisfied human needs. Generally these creative persons emerge in periods of social tension, when men feel bewildered and impotent. Moses and the prophets among the Hebrews, Zoroaster among the Persians, Gautama among the Hindus, Confucius and Lao-tsze among the Chinese, Jesus and Paul in the Roman Empire, Mohammed among the Arabs, illustrate how creative personalities undertake to correct and reapply religious beliefs and practices to the new elements of some culture.

Religion and Social Behavior

Each of them was more than an isolated teacher. Around each arose a group which has had direct social influence. Because of them civilizations have been affected and to some extent remade.

A comparison of such religious movements within social orders will disclose characteristics strikingly similar. The influence of all new religious groups is proportionate to the extent to which they participate in the social process which has given rise to tensions showing the weaknesses of the older religion. Sometimes this integration of the new religious group with the total cultural group gives new direction to social change; in other cases its influence is checked at the point of adjustment to social conditions. Each stratum of economic development of different peoples has precipitated essentially the same moral code. Honesty, chastity, respect for property rights, limitation in taking human life, become divinely sanctioned elements in each civilization as it reaches a certain level of economic development. If this economic life suffers no further change the religious codes are judged sufficient. When such changes come, however, a religion either progresses or decays. Gen-

Christianity and Social Process

erally speaking, therefore, as a matter of self-protection a religion is opposed to social change. Even the reforming group tends to become orthodox. The vitality of a religious group can be judged by its capacity to produce nonconformist groups devoted to further extension of the religion's ideals and basic characteristics to new social situations.

VII

Champions of a religion are likely to claim absolute values for their own religion. The defenders of Christianity have been accustomed to assert that it is the only religion; that all others are false. Similar convictions are expressed by the adherents of other religions. Today tolerance is becoming more widespread, but tolerance does not necessarily imply that one is open-minded as to the truth of that which he tolerates. A comparative study would seem to show that while all religions have the same function, they are not all equally efficient. It is not unlike the matter of food; all food has the same function but not all foods are equally digestible. If they are to be anything more than "opiates of the people" the practices and institutions of a religion must not only conserve existing values, but they must give moral direction to forces by which a social order is being changed. Such a creative participation in social process will be subject to the general laws of social psychology. Neither individuals nor groups can be disregarded.

A proper understanding of the Christian religion necessitates the recognition of these facts. Its content and its influence can be understood only as it is approached historically and from the point of view of social psychology. Such an approach is neither theological nor apologetic. Christianity is as truly a religion and as genuinely illustrates the relation of a religion to a social process as does Hinduism or Mohammedanism. Historically speaking, Christianity is a religion which constitutes within Western civilization a social movement characterized by institutions and beliefs peculiarly its own. It has, like every other religion, owed its influence to a social structure quite as truly as to a system of doctrines. Yet these doctrines have expressed values which the movement as a whole has claimed to express and apply. The relationship of Christianity to a social process should be studied historically, therefore, to discover both these values and their influence upon that process.

II

CHRISTIANITY AS AN ASPECT OF WESTERN CIVILIZATION

THERE is a cynical epigram to the effect that Christianity has not failed, because it has never been tried. Such an epigram, like all its fellows, is a half-truth calculated to irritate those who believe the other half-truth. It is certainly not historical. It implies that Christianity is to be identified with the Sermon on the Mount or some other formula of Jesus. It may be that this is what Christianity ought to be, but it is not what the Christian religion as an element of history has been. As a religion it is not to be identified with a literature or a system of doctrines. These are related to Christianity as the Bill of Rights and the Act of Settlement are to the constitutional history of Great Britain. Ideals cannot work apart from idealists, and idealists are to a greater or

Christianity and Social Process

less extent the creatures of their own time. Historically and realistically considered, Christianity is the religion of people who say they are Christians.

This is more definite than it sounds. Persons who call themselves Christians have regarded Jesus Christ as their Saviour. Christianity as a religion is the religious movement centering about the person and teaching of its founder. It originated in the Near East, expanded into Europe, passed to America. In our own day it has spread with other elements of Western civilization to Asia and Africa. In all religious groups into which it has been differentiated it has bred true to itself. Persons who would call themselves Christians have regarded Jesus as a revealer of God and Saviour of man. In all the customs and institutions which different groups of Christians have established, in all the doctrines by which they rationalize their religious experience and hopes, a belief in Jesus has been central.

I

The New Testament makes it plain that Christianity did not start as a philosophy, but as a social

Christianity and Western Civilization

movement. The Messianic hope which Jesus was believed to fulfill was sublimated Jewish nationalism. A new Jewish kingdom was to be founded by God; indeed, was already existing in heaven. Those who prepared to join it when it was established constituted a distinct group. They had no system of doctrine, they did not break with the Jewish nation or the Jewish religion. They had faith that Jesus, who had gone to heaven, would return to inaugurate the new kingdom in which their leaders would sit upon thrones judging the twelve tribes of Israel. As the group expanded by the addition of non-Jewish members, the Jewish limitations of this hope were abandoned, but its supernatural elements were retained. In this extension of his significance, however, Jesus remained the divine Saviour. The Christian group carried over the theistic conceptions of the prophets but abandoned their nationalist hopes. The satisfactions which they sought in their new religion and the means by which they were to be gained were centered around deliverance from death. The customs and institutions which they developed constituted a technique for such deliverance. Baptism

Christianity and Social Process

and the Eucharist were regarded as channels by which the saving grace of God regenerated and sustained the believer. Moral living was to be expected on the part of the members of the group, but it was not the means of salvation. Within the group there developed, however, distinct moral ideas which were centered around the person and teaching of the founder. Its test of membership was not moral, but belief in supernatural elements which were finally codified in what became known as the Apostles' Creed. Only those who could profess such faith could be admitted to the sacred mystery of the Eucharist. Those who violated conventional moral codes were subject to discipline, which in the course of years became organized into the new technique of penance. This was regarded also as a sacrament through which grace came. As the Christian community grew more powerful, marriage also became a sacrament. The same is true of certain church practices. The group thus gained in ability to direct itself and individual morality.

In this development of Christianity from a phase of Judaism to an independent religion, the

Christianity and Western Civilization

influence of contemporary ideals and practices is clearly seen. The movement ceased to be Jewish and became Græco-Roman as its Hellenist members brought into it current philosophies, religious rites, business practices, and social customs. Their supreme motives were, however, drawn from their loyalty to Jesus as a Saviour. Philosophically they sought to establish him as an object of worship without abandoning monotheism. Morally they made—often unintelligently—his example supreme.

The emergence of doctrines was inevitable in an age forbidden by authority to give attention to social and political reform. Almost immediately doctrine became an agent of group solidarity. Within the new community there naturally developed differences of opinion. These differences resulted in rival groupings which threatened the movement itself. From the struggle between these groups there arose authoritative dogma. Orthodoxy was the belief of the victorious party. But these struggles did not touch loyalty to Jesus as the center of hope and faith. They were rather concerned to show in different ways what seemed

Christianity and Social Process

the real meaning of this loyalty. Paradoxically, men quarreled over reasons for what they all believed. There was no difference, for instance, between the Arians and the Athanasians over the saving work of Jesus; their differences lay in the way of vindicating such a belief. Throughout the entire history of the Christian movement this controversy between those who agree on a basic faith has gone on. The Christian movement has been, therefore, less subject to division than to differentiation. As Mohammedans say that Allah is one and Mohammed is his prophet, so practically all the groups of Christians say that their God is one substance and Jesus Christ is the one Saviour.

But despite its centering on such loyalty the Christian movement has not erected the teaching of Jesus into a law. Jesus himself rather than his teaching has been the center of Christianity. He has been a Saviour-God for millions. Creeds and Confessions have been drawn up, but they have not been all of the religion. Whatever may have been the differences in the doctrines with which Christians have justified their faith in Jesus, there has been no difference of opinion among them as to the basic moral quality of the religion he founded. Men ought to live as he would have them live. There has been no division among the Christians as to the ideals represented by the life, teachings, and sacrificial death of Jesus. Christianity on its theological side has been a more or less intelligent vindication of ideals for human behavior. The ecumenical creeds have taken such morality for granted and have not mentioned it. Dogma may have kept groups belligerent, but the ideals of Christian morality have never been divisive except as they have been affected by asceticism appropriated from non-Christian religions. And the most ascetic medieval practices never questioned the validity of the moral precepts of Jesus.

Doubtless the chief reasons for such unanimous demand for moral excellence are the divine character ascribed to Jesus as the incarnation of God and the fact that he made love the sole condition of entrance into the Kingdom of God. For he himself established no cult or independent religion. The way in which to become like God, he taught, was to love one's enemies. His religion was not mystical, but morally active. Men could expect divine forgiveness only as they forgave others.

These teachings have always furnished the absolute moral ideal for the Christian movement. Despite men's readiness to regard them as impracticable, to compromise them, and to adjust them to actual situations, their influence has always been felt. There has always been discussion within Christian groups as to the conditions under which men could enjoy Christ's salvation, but never as to the attitudes that are Christlike. Morality, not metaphysics, was in truth the heart of the new religious movement Christ founded.

It therefore is necessary to abandon the conception of Christianity as merely a set of doctrines and to see it as it actually is, the religious behavior of a continuous, on-going social movement, a phase of the social process which characterized the history of western Europe and which from there extended over the rest of the world. Except in the case of certain religious fraternities Christians have

Christianity and Western Civilization

never undertaken to organize social life according to a literal application of teaching of Jesus. As members of an institutionalized movement they have found themselves repeatedly confronting conditions born of economic or political forces and as a form of social behavior the general character and methods of Christianity, like those of other religions, have been determined by people who composed a social order. The history of Christianity is the history of Christians. When a social order was imperial the religion was imperial. In a feudal state theology grew feudal; when nations arose, Christians organized national churches and theologies; when democracy emerged, Christian groups became democratic. Yet these changes were never complete. Inherited Christian institutions and teachings were preserved in various orthodoxies. Changes were by way of the differentiation rather than destruction of the past. The development of the Christian movement has been and still is, one might say, a biological process in which an organism is both modified by changes in its environment and simultaneously changes the environment.

Christianity and Social Process

II

That the Christian religion should have survived the social cataclysm which destroyed the Roman Empire was largely due to its being a social movement possessing institutional vitality. Other religions, like those of Mithra and classical paganism, failed in no small part for lack of such institutional integrity. Civilization had to begin over again in western Europe. The invaders from the north knew nothing of literature or Christianity or gentleness. They had a lingering respect for the decadent empire they were destroying, but none the less they destroyed it. They thus set up conditions in which the Christian church preserved almost the only vestiges of earlier days. The Christian movement was not responsible for the brutality of the barbarian Christians any more than it was responsible for the conditions which developed in what we roughly call the Dark Ages. Their moral attitude was furnished poor techniques by a crude civilization to which they belonged. Many of the beliefs and practices of ignorant and cruel people persisted in the Christian group.

Christianity and Western Civilization

None the less the religion of western Europe was the Christian religion—that is to say, a social behavior which organized practices, ideals, and teachings believed to center about Jesus. Though he was often sadly misunderstood, and that which was accidental in his life made authoritative, he was the ground of hope for salvation.

Christianity, however, is not to be identified with Western civilization. A nation can be called Christian only in the sense that its dominant religion is Christianity. Western civilization and Christianty are very different. No single element of a social process can account for its changes. The Christian religion is only one of the forces that made Western civilization what it became.

The boundaries of Latin Christianity and those of the area within which Western civilization developed are practically identical. The reason is plain. The people who constituted the Christian movement in western Europe from the fall of the Roman Empire to the beginning of the nineteenth century were the same persons who waged wars, built castles, carried on the commerce, organized monarchies, established capitalism and democracy, made science a handmaid of mankind, and established colleges and universities. It is loose thinking that sets Christianity as something complete, compact, and independent, over against this highly complicated social process. The ideals for which the church stood could find expression only in the atmosphere which existed in different lands and times. Because of the influences of other social forces the Christian religion was remodeled. In its original form it had possessed no priesthood, no philosophy, no peculiar customs. Its most sacred practices, baptism and the Lord's Supper, were not peculiar to itself, but had meaning because of what they were believed to represent. Unlike Judaism, which was developing contemporaneously, Christianity had no moral or ethnic code. Its moral ideals as set forth both by Jesus and by Paul were general and personal, without detailed statutory application. But in the course of time the Christian movement, like other religious movements, organized a cult and a system of theology. In so doing it embodied the behavior, institutions, and thought of the peoples who accepted it. It is, of course, idle to speculate as to

Christianity and Western Civilization

what might have taken place if Christianity had not moved westward to become the dominant religion in the Roman Empire. If we can judge from the history of Buddhism, its intellectual and institutional development would have been different. The behavior patterns of the West were not the behavior patterns of the East. There was, in the East, no imperial unity to develop an imperialistic church like that of Rome. There was no incursion of Teutonic peoples to reconstitute the Christian movement both ethnically, politically, and socially. A different set of social customs and institutions would have conditioned the organization of Christian groups and churches. The only way to understand correctly the Christian religion is to recognize it as the religious aspect of the evolution of Western civilization.

III

In such a study of the place of Christianity in the development of a civilization the church will be seen to have been one of many factors cooperating to develop the *mores* of a time and a country. Recognition of this fact will assist in a

Christianity and Social Process

fair estimate of its success and failure as a moral guide. It would be incorrect to attribute social progress toward the ideal implicit in the Christian movement to the church alone. *Post hoc* is not always identical with *propter hoc*. Social trends of many sorts are observable in the relation of groups, and the church has never been exempt from their influence. Even its claim to supernatural powers and to being the most effective if not the sole agency of divine grace does not obscure its actual relationship with the other factors of a civilization. Its influence must be felt as one element of a general synthesis and its participation with other agencies of the social process as one of reciprocal influence.

I use the word church in a very general way to represent organized Christianity. Such a use is liable to misinterpretation, but I know of no other single term that so clearly embodies the fact that Christians have uniformly set up coöperative action out from which have sprung various types of organizations. The Christian movement has been a movement of groups. Such organizations have always been centered around convictions concern-

Christianity and Western Civilization

ing Jesus as a Saviour. It is sometimes said that if a man is religious he may be indifferent to theology. Indeed, theology just now is rather on the defensive. But a study of the Christian movement gives no support to the treatment of beliefs as detachable from a religion as a form of social behavior. On the contrary, they have been means by which the solidarity and basic attitudes of the Christian communities have been preserved. The Christian movement, at its start, was not primarily interested in ethics. It was the group of those who attached superhuman position and later deity to its founder. Men were not saved because they were good, but they were under obligation to be good because they were saved. Faith in Jesus was the center of group solidarity, but within this group new behavior was developed. As the movement threw out new groups, creeds and confessions have been organized in no small measure to exclude from these Christian bodies those who were not in sympathy with their particular beliefs. As a result the Christian community has become unique in religious history. Other religions have priesthoods, monastic orders, national and ethnic loyalties. But

Christianity and Social Process

in the Christian churches there is a homogeneity that has not been destroyed by their differentiation. Orthodoxies have been conservers of group solidarity, perpetuating basic beliefs and moral ideals and behavior.

There has, however, been no uniformity in Christian groups. Permanent values have been expressed in formulas and in institutions contemporary with their organization and accepted by members of the groups themselves. Thus, from western Europe, where imperialistic practices and institutions were creative, the Christians organized themselves in the pattern of imperialism. On the other hand, in the eastern half of Europe and in the Near East, where Roman imperialism had been superimposed upon nationalities, there was no unity in organized Christianity. In several respects the halves of the Christian movement differed to such an extent that each regarded the other as schismatic. Later, when new European states were being organized, in those which had not been within the ancient Roman Empire the Christian churches became phases of the individual states subject to national self-direction. Protestant-

Christianity and Western Civilization

ism took the form of state churches. With the rise of the commercial class and of democracy other churches, not national in character, were organized on the democratic model.

IV

While the Christian movement preserves unchangeable values, the word church stands for different sorts of administrative control. As a general term it can be used only to represent Christianity in its group aspects. There has never been any ecclesiastical organization of all Christians, although the thought of such a single organization has always been present in some minds, and different bodies have claimed to represent what has always been believed by true Christians everywhere. But even those bodies which claim catholicity do not agree among themselves as to organization and doctrines. In the case of Protestants it was natural, therefore, for the church to be spoken of as invisible, something which exists in heaven, but does not exist on the earth. Continuous differentiation into state churches, denominations, and sects has characterized the Protestant

Christianity and Social Process

movement from the sixteenth to the twentieth century.

Nor do churches represent all those who in some way or other accept Jesus as teacher and seek to embody those values which Christianity as a social movement represents. The organized and unorganized elements of the Christian movement sometimes have been in mutual opposition. As organized institutions churches have sometimes favored, but quite as often opposed, the changes which their own ideals have worked within a social process.

For an understanding of the relation of the Christian religion to the development of Western civilization attention must be given to the methods by which Christian groups have developed the *mores* of their members and made their influence felt beyond their own limits. In general such a process followed the laws of group interpenetration.

v

The influence of a church upon social evolution in the West has been that of one social group

Christianity and Western Civilization

among others. No church has always been unqualifiedly in favor of progress toward its own ideals. Control of its influence and power has usually been in the hands of those to whom change in the *status quo* has appeared dangerous. The tendency toward the maintenance of existing conditions has too often been seen in the action of ecclesiastics. A church under their influence has favored existing institutions and has become an institution, an end in itself. Not a few churches have sought to maintain their integrity by the severe repression of all nonconformity. Persecution has usually resulted from the intimate coöperation of an established church and a government.

But to center attention upon such un-Christian activities of Christian bodies is to overlook the fact that within them individuals and minority groups have been inspired to appreciate the significance of the value the movement embodies. Thanks to them, while the churches have initiated few, if any, radical reforms, they have served in some measure to give moral direction to changes within a social process.

At times such influence has been indistinguish-

Christianity and Social Process

able from a social process itself. At other times, however, the ideals of personal rights and brotherhood have been explicitly preached. Especially has this been the case as religion and politics have been separated in the development of democracy. But the directive influence of the moral ideals of the Christian movement on social process has been opportunist. They have impregnated specific social readjustments rather than a social order. They have never been revolutionary. Thus in the Roman Empire, although the church did not attempt to destroy slavery as a social institution, by making human values superior to economic, it gave moral impetus to the economic transformation that made slavery unprofitable. It was hard for a Christian to own a brother in Christ. Slaves were members of the Christian communities, and were thus given a status that in the nature of the case tended to destroy slavery as an institution as well as to furnish new group relationships for those who were freed by their masters because of the growing poverty of the Empire.

But the Christian movement was to act as a ferment in a much greater series of social changes.

Christianity and Western Civilization

The thousand years that elapsed between the so-called fall of the Roman Empire and the emergence of the modern states of western Europe were an epitome of the course of human history. A civilization had to be established. Fortunately, in the process through which this was accomplished, western Europe had assets which primitive man lacked. Vestiges of a civilization which carried Christian institutions survived. The church preserved some elements of the literature of the Roman world, as well as many of its administrative habits. The Holy Roman Empire, although it was destined to become a political ghost to be laid by Napoleon, during the medieval period conserved a grand ideal: human society was to be unified under the control of the emperor and the pope, who were responsible as vicegerents to Christ himself. The history of Europe shows how incompatible such an ideal was with actual human ambitions and methods, but it illustrated the position which the church occupied in politics. Practically all the great statesmen were ecclesiastics. It was they who conducted diplomacy and organized governments. Economic and political policies

Christianity and Social Process

were given enthusiasm by appeals to religious fanaticism. Usually inspired or justified by religious enthusiasm, crusades seeking to recover the Holy Land for Christendom became social forces in western Europe which hastened the end of feudalism, developed the commercial importance of towns, and laid the foundations for the readjustments of the sixteenth and seventeenth centuries. In this process the church responded to and to some extent directed the new conditions. Universities were founded in which generations of men were given the discipline of an education in which there was little science but much logical acuteness. There is no parallel to the systematic, although historically indifferent, intellectual processes of the schoolmen, practically every one of whom was an ecclesiastic. The students in these universities became the lawyers and statesmen of Europe—another illustration of the way in which the Christian movement has provided persons who act as a ferment in social processes which the movement itself has not originated.

Equally appreciable was the influence of Christianity upon art. Community interest and mu-

Christianity and Western Civilization

nicipal pride found expression in cathedrals and churches. Painting was for centuries almost exclusively concerned with religious subjects like altar pieces, windows, and statues, intended to assist worship. It was only when the expanding spirit of the Renaissance came under the influence of classicism that ecclesiastical art found a rival in secular art.

VI

Thus from whatever point of human interest the history of the Christian movement in the West is observed, it appears as an aspect of that process of cross-fertilization of groups from which Western civilization emerged. It shared the limitations and retrogressions as well as the progress of that process. It appropriated the thought forms and social practices of each destructive and constructive period. As an increasingly organized and then differentiated movement it was never alien to the world of which it was a part. It utilized the fears of the ignorant and the intellectual capacities of the cultured. It organized an imperial church, state churches, free churches, and non-ecclesiastical

Christianity and Social Process

groups, each expressing the social mind of a stage in the developing civilization. But it was more than a passive participant in the social process. While it initiated few social reforms, it supplied ideals and inhibitions for social forces resident in an evolving civilization. What these socially preserved and applied values were we need to consider.

III

THE MORAL NATURE OF THE CHRISTIAN RELIGION

THE historical study of Christianity as a social behavior constituting one aspect of Western civilization involves the discovery of the values which it has conserved. It also helps one to understand how the ideals of a religious movement are obscured and even abandoned because of its zeal for self-preservation.

The church has of late been subjected to excessive criticism and made the scapegoat for social evils. Much of this criticism is justifiable, but much more of it is due to the inability of the critics to look at things from the point of view of process. It is easy to treat Christianity absolutely and civilization relatively. Over against the injustice and ineptitude of a social order facing unprece-

Christianity and Social Process

dented economic and political tasks is set some saying of Jesus. The fact that such a saying has not been literally observed is regarded either as an evidence of its inapplicability to group action or as an indictment of mid-Victorian sentimentalism. Such criticism ignores the fact that a religion is not a literature or a memory, but the behavior of persons participating in various social groups who profess to be loyal to a movement which embodies ideals. To judge the efficiency of Christianity by pointing out the contradiction between its ideals and human performance is certainly far from a scientific method. Indifference to social process begets denunciatory dogmatism. Coercion and terror seem then the only implements for furthering idealism.

A saner method is to discover whether as a social behavior Christianity conserves values which affect social evolution. Right and wrong, moral and immoral, are terms with which the unhistorical mind loves to juggle. But the concrete effects of any movement within a social order are the real criterion of its worth. Its institutions and practices can be judged by the extent to which they

Moral Nature of the Christian Religion

implement its ideals and affect the social order. If one is to estimate the share of the Christian religion in the social process of the West one must, therefore, discover what values it furthers as its essential characteristics. The extent and the ways of influence exerted by these values as they have been expressed in social behavior can then be discovered.

I

As has already been indicated, the Christian movement has perpetuated values which originated in an estimate of the life and teaching of Jesus. These values have been formulated in theological systems which groups of Christians have produced. Such systems are functional rather than final. They are ways of rationalizing loyalty to the values implicit in the Christian movement when questioned or threatened by successive social tensions. Christian doctrines originated in past social needs. That they were treated as statutes was due to the dominant social minds which they represented. To outgrow a doctrine is not to deny the value it may express. The first duty of the

Christianity and Social Process

historian of Christianity is to discover the influence of social situations in the organization of its dogmas.

The development of orthodox theology resembles that of common law. Social practices in England antedate statutory enactment. They were ways in which the community believed its members should act. As new conditions arose these social convictions were organized as law by courts and legislative bodies. In such legislation the original experiences and ideals persisted to such a degree that common law characterizes an English social order wherever found. And only such an order. Continental law preserved the legal conceptions and administration of Rome just as English law carried forward practices and ideals of those who were never Romanized. The development of the various religions furnishes illustrations of a similar projection of the experiences of different groups into formulas. Each has its own characteristics because it has its own history. As different legal systems have the same function while differing in technique, so various religions, while all seeking to establish some help-gaining relations

Moral Nature of the Christian Religion

between God and man, have been characterized by different techniques. The outstanding characteristic of the Christian religion is that its technique is a morality. Orthodox Christian theology might be described as a system of sublimated moral relations. How different this is from metaphysics or philosophy is to be seen in the fact that its doctrines are social patterns by which relations between men are used to set forth the relations of men and God. Although philosophies have been used to justify and explain its contents, theology developed as a rationalization of social behavior rather than as philosophical ideas. One has only to recall the many elements of orthodox theology to see that Christian doctrines are analogies in which faith in Jesus as the Saviour has been integrated with different stages of the social process from which Western civilization has evolved. These analogies have been drawn from social practices approved by a contemporary morality. The very vocabulary of dogma makes this plain. Practically all its terms are derived from the political and legal practices by which a social order sought to preserve itself from disorder. The ecumenical creeds contain only one metaphysical word, "consubstantial," and even this has always been interpreted through the analogy of "begetting." One might indeed say that orthodox theology is a scenario of a cosmic drama or the outline of a cosmic epic like Milton's *Paradise Lost* and *Paradise Regained*. Its basic conception is that of sovereignty such as men of New Testament and patristic times accepted in the Roman Empire. In its doctrine of the atonement there lived not only the practice of sacrifice of pre-Christian religions, but the feudal practice of satisfying injured dignity by some form of composition. The absolute monarchy of seventeenth-century Europe reappears in the decrees and covenants, punishments and pardons, of Calvinism. In fact, whatever has seemed to be an ultimate ground of moral relations in any social order has been regarded as an attribute of the Deity in Christian theology. Tested by Biblical ideals, these patterns have grown into dogmas enforced rather than defined as conditions of membership within a Christian group.

Moral Nature of the Christian Religion

II

The values discovered by the analysis of the doctrinal patterns thus derived from the social process in the West are intrinsically personal and moral rather than speculative. With them rather than the doctrines in which they have been expressed the Christian challenges every type of mechanistic interpretation of life and every attempt to reduce a world of men to a mass of self-indulgent brutes. Whatever be the patterns in which they are expressed, these values are implicit in Christian theologies developed in all grades of human culture. They are mind-sets of a continuous social group seeking better and more hopeful living because of loyalty to Jesus as a revealer of the relation of God and man.

When stripped of their patterns these values are as follows:

1. The cosmos is not mechanistic, but instinct with personality-producing activities. These forces have had a part in the evolution of humanity and must be treated as elements in the environment in which men must live. That is what Christians

mean when they say that there is a God in whom they live and move and have their being. For the word *God* is the term which we use to describe those personality-producing activities of the cosmos which constitute a part of the environment conditioning the development of humanity and with which men must live personally.

2. The God of law is a God of love. This is the heart of the teaching of Jesus and it is this which every theological system has endeavored to make tenable and helpful. If difficulty in holding this belief sprang from casting the relation of God and man in political analogies, it was met by corollaries drawn from the same analogies, and God's son, Jesus Christ, was regarded as bearing the punishment which otherwise would have fallen upon humanity.

The modern world has outgrown these patterns because it has a more intelligent conception of punishment. God is more than a sovereign, and his relations with the universe are not those of a seventeenth-century king. New patterns are being used. As men gain in intelligence they better understand cosmic activities and learn how to control

Moral Nature of the Christian Religion

or to adjust themselves to them. The same activities that have made us personal will aid us in our attempt to be more personal. Christian doctrines do not undertake to decide why we have such a universe as we have, but they undertake to show how men can live superior to all the mechanisms which they have inherited, even though such living involves sacrifice. The word sin stands, therefore, for something more than disobedience to formal divine commands. It is a moral and personal maladjustment with cosmic activities which must and can be overcome if men's personal needs are to be met.

3. Personal values are superior to all others. It is this conviction that dignifies the more or less directed zeal of ascetics and Puritans. The effort to express this conviction in actual social relations has varied with the intelligence and the social structure of different periods. One could not expect a society whose very existence depended upon the maintenance of feudal institutions to be democratic.

But the Christian church, conditioned by the crudities and brutalities of men who were only

Christianity and Social Process

with difficulty raising themselves from barbarism, showed that humanity had worth, and offered heaven to the poor as well as to the rich.

4. Human progress implies and demands the democratizing of privilege. This is the real meaning of love as Christ taught and embodied it. In the effort to give rather than to get justice, the Christian religion has been immensely aided by having its ideal dramatized in the life and death of its founder. The loyalty of Christians to him will be measured by their endeavor to reproduce in their world-order the same attitude which he embodied in his. Love furnishes the motive, and science the technique of a new stage in social evolution.

5. Kindliness and service assure help-gaining adjustment with the personality-producing activities of the universe. Such a fact is expressed in the human analogy of father and son so characteristic of Jesus' teaching. An unforgiving man had no chance of divine forgiveness. But the truth is independent of the particular analogy. It can be viewed as the dependence of an organism upon that element of its environment which has de-

Moral Nature of the Christian Religion

termined its most recent stage. A water-breathing animal which has become air-breathing must live in the air. An animal that has become human must live in harmony with the activities that have made him personal.

The Christian religion, like all techniques of social relations, uses anthropomorphic analogies, but the relationship itself is more than anthropomorphism. Whoever can accept evolution as the most likely hypothesis by which to organize our knowledge of the emergence of humanity will recognize the inevitability of this Christian position. Instead of seeking a de-individualized union with infinity or an emotionless Nirvana, it looks toward and develops a more personal individual.

6. To such development death is an episode, not an end. We can abandon all the crude pictures of heaven, hell, and purgatory, and yet see that they were endeavors to set forth a profound probability. An individual person whose center of life is beyond the control of animal survivals and who is at one with the personality-producing activities of the cosmos may expect some new and less animal mode of life as the next step in evolution.

Christianity and Social Process

The moral significance of the Christian religion is embodied in formulas of its churches. Each of its beliefs involves moral action. To regard Christianity merely as a collection of esoteric truths which have no bearing on social conduct is unhistorically to transform it from a religion to a philosophy. The Christianity of history is to be found in the attitudes and behavior of a continuous group which because of its loyalty to Jesus Christ has gained assurance that its members are to have a more personal and happier life. To justify this assurance Christians of different periods have shown its consistency with philosophy, politics, and in fact any element of life not itself subject to question, but its ultimate basis is its efficiency to socialize the values conserved in Christian groups participating in a social process.

III

Radical morality needs religious sanction if men are to make voluntarily the sacrifices it involves. Unless God is love, there is little reason to believe love is a practical basis upon which to build a social order. Men will prefer coercion. The teachers

Moral Nature of the Christian Religion

of the church have been handicapped in presenting the love of God by contemporary social practices. Saint Bernard, it is true, did argue earnestly that love is not an attribute, but of the substance of the deity, but the theologians have insisted that even when God forgave certain of the human race there was some ulterior motive in the act. Augustine and Anselm say this ultimate motive is God's desire to restore the perfect number of the angels, which had been injured by the defection of Satan and his followers. Thomas Aquinas is influenced by philosophical conceptions of the Deity derived from Aristotle. The Protestant theologians say with a distinguished teacher that God must be just, he may be merciful. But even in the latter case the claims of justice had to be satisfied before the divine love could express itself. This satisfaction was wrought by the atoning work of the Son of God. Thus the pattern of a loving Father in Christ's teaching has been subordinated to that of the feudal lord and absolute sovereign.

True, since the passing of the absolute monarchy and the rise of democracy, the patterns with which the divine attitude to mankind has been expressed,

Christianity and Social Process

give more importance to the love of the Heavenly Father. The older doctrines of the atonement are taught, but the sharp antagonism between the attitude toward the humanity of God the Father and that of God the Son has been decidedly softened even within the circle of orthodoxy. The divine justice is being tempered by divine mercy, and the fatherhood of God is becoming increasingly the fatherliness of God.

That this change in theological thought has sometimes grown sentimental can hardly be denied. Sentimentality has always been an aspect of a civilization which, like the Western, has not coordinated love and efficiency. It was inevitable that the love of God should sometimes have been so described as to appear hardly more than divine good nature. But even in the analogies and patterns with which Christian teachers have set forth the central thought of divine relationship, it is clear that God's love is something more than liking. It includes action looking toward the welfare of others, which does not disregard basic moral obligations as a social order conceives them. The Deity in Christian doctrine is neither captious nor

Moral Nature of the Christian Religion

irascible. He is not subject to the whims of despotic rulers; his love, like his law, is moral. He does not need to be placated; he needs only to express his love of sinners in ways which do not shock the moral idealism of his followers. In every doctrine of the atonement God takes the initiative; God's own sacrificial act discloses His moral integrity. Doctrinal patterns are relative to historical situations, but values remain constant.

The validity of this religious basis of love in the Christian movement has not been unquestioned. There are those who say that love of our fellows requires no divine sanction; that men, so to speak, may be brothers without a divine Father. Such humanistic philosophy is not that of Christianity. It does not properly treat doctrines as functional. So far as the Christian religion is concerned, the logical basis of altruism is religious. Jesus taught that men became children of the Heavenly Father by being like Him in their loving treatment of their fellows. Throughout the course of Christian history, despite the crudities and even brutalities of patterns derived from a crude and brutal social order, the church has always insisted that the love

Christianity and Social Process

of God was a motive for the love of men. The social psychologist cannot disregard the suggestion of the social attitude of sacrifice implicit in the Cross. Despite the evil men who have exploited the church, despite the uncritical appropriation of unworthy practices as the expression of the Christian spirit, the ideal which the Christian movement has always embodied has been that of likeness to the Heavenly Father. If the Son is of the same substance as the Father, the Father is of the same character as the Son. Whenever in the development of organized Christian groups faith in a God who not only loves but is lovable has been replaced by the fear of a God who needs to be appeased, Christianity has lost its influence as the leaven of love.

In thus speaking of God as loving, we are of course speaking anthropomorphically. But such a method is inevitable and must be regarded as instrumental rather than as metaphysical. Religion as distinct from philosophy will always be anthropomorphic in that men attempt to set up relations with cosmic activities in the same way that they set up relations between persons. To speak of

Moral Nature of the Christian Religion

God as loving is the religious way of pointing out that there is in the universe a tendency to coördinate various units of activity into new combinations. Electrons combine into atoms, atoms into molecules, molecules into colloids, and ultimately all these units into organisms. But the nucleating, coördinating process does not stop at that point. The organisms themselves must not only be at one with the environment, but they tend to form social groups. Animals run in packs and mankind organizes societies. For the individual, therefore, to live as if such coördinating and grouping tendency were not in the nature of things is to run counter to the constructive activity of the universe. Religiously we say that he is running counter to the will of God. That is to say, from either the scientific or the religious approach, we must conclude that the personal welfare of the individual can be furthered only coöperatively. Such coöperation, if moral, is the expression of the cosmic coördinating principle on the level of personality. The organization of human groups makes possible achievement of values inaccessible to subhuman activity. Love may not even be liking for

Christianity and Social Process

those one loves, but it is a moral activity at one with cosmic activity. How can we doubt that it is a practicable basis upon which to organize society?

Humanity, however, does not yet believe wholeheartedly that it is. Centuries of war and social oppression have left their vestiges in Western civilization. To many persons love seems to be effeminacy or effeminate sentimentality. The strong man is preferred to the loving man. Men who hold to the philosophy of force and the will to power naturally discount the ideals of the Christian religion. Self-sacrifice in the interest of others, the readiness to democratize one's advantages in the interest of others who share the social situation, is certainly far away from traditional human policies. It has been far easier to believe that members of some social unity, whether it be that of a family or of a nation, can be coerced into doing the will of a master. The social order of the West does not yet embody the moral ideal of coöperation or recognize the common rights of all its members. The moral values of the Christian movement must again be adjusted to a social tension if they are to be efficiently expressed in social behavior.

Moral Nature of the Christian Religion

IV

To recognize the values which a group conserves is not to describe the social behavior of that group or to understand just how it affects a social process. This is particularly true of religions. In them antiquity is often identified with sanctity. That which has always been practiced is abandoned with apprehension lest the deity should punish the neglect. All religions therefore have perpetuated practices which originated in a more primitive stage of culture. Christianity as a historical movement is no exception to this generalization. Quite independently of the values they express, the doctrines and practices of earlier days have been preserved by Christian communities. Christianity as the social behavior of men and women has been very different from the theological formulations of ecclesiastical bodies and scholars. When once social practices have become an inheritance they can be abandoned only by something akin to a revolution. The supreme position accorded to Mary had become so universal in the Eastern half of the Empire that even a churchman like Nes-

Christianity and Social Process

torius could not prevent the use of the term, "mother of God." With the collapse of Western civilization during the barbarian invasions the polytheism of the Roman religion reappeared in the appeal to innumerable saints, most of whom continued the activities of some god or goddess. Monotheism was maintained officially, but the religious practices of the Christian group were—as can be seen from the pages of Gregory of Tours— marked by crass superstition. In the course of time some of these practices were rationalized in doctrine and in a way coördinated with what might be called major Christianity. They thus became as truly elements of historical Christianity as the ideals which the movement inherited from Jesus. Successive reforms have never seriously affected these aspects of the Christian movement except by way of schism and the organization of groups which have been opposed and in many cases persecuted.

This differentiation of religious groups has characterized Western civilization, but beyond the emergence of relatively unimportant sects it is not observable in Eastern Christianity since the pa-

Moral Nature of the Christian Religion

tristic period. There are doubtless many reasons for the static quality of the Eastern churches, but changes in Western Christianity have sprung from social tensions. Repeatedly in the West individuals protested against what seemed to them to be objectionable religious practices and teachings, only to be suppressed, their followers subjected to persecution and forced to exist, if at all, as secret groups. When, however, the new economic, political, and intellectual forces began to find expression in the sixteenth century, a religious revolt was practicable. At one time it looked as if Western Europe might break with the papacy, but political considerations and dynastic ambitions finally restricted any radical religious reorganization due to these new social forces, to countries where there were few traces of Roman civilization. In the differentiation of the Protestant state churches the doctrinal element of the Christian movement as organized by Roman theologians continued, but practices which were regarded as not justified by the Scriptures were abandoned. There does not seem to have been any abandonment, however, of the belief that the chief function of the Christian

Christianity and Social Process

movement was to enable men to avoid hell and enjoy heaven. Like the church fathers, the Protestant teachers did not undertake to extend the Christian values to social institutions, but limited their efforts to conventional individual morality. Since the state controlled the organization of national churches it was the duty of the churches to support the state. Protestants might reject five of the sacraments, might believe in the priesthood of all believers who were to be acquitted at the coming judgment through their faith alone, but their Confessions were political documents. The Wars of Religion and the Thirty Years' War were the natural outcome of such conditions. Loyalty to Jesus did not prevent ecclesiastical and political conflict. The basic moral and religious values which Catholics and Protestants alike profess were submerged by the passions of men who thought it wrong to steal and commit adultery, but had no moral sensitiveness as to the rights of peasants or the massacre of non-combatants in a war for territorial expansion.

One chief reason for this tragical inconsistency is undoubtedly the official organization of Chris-

Moral Nature of the Christian Religion

tian groups. The extent to which this has proceeded is great. The Roman Catholic Church is worldwide in its extent, but it includes a large number of fraternities and sisterhoods, charitable and educational institutions, which are efficiently organized and subordinated to local or papal control. Until the rise of modern states the Catholic Church was the one organization which, although recognizing national and even local differences, was superior to political boundaries. As the representative of God on earth it controlled individual morality, and to a very considerable extent social customs and political policies.

What the Catholic Church thus exhibits on a vast scale the other churches have exhibited on a limited scale. In the same proportion as the solidarity of a religious group develops, its maintenance becomes of paramount importance. Loyalty to its beliefs and institutions overshadows the recognition of its function to the individual. Heresy has been more severely punished than social lapses. Indeed, religious organizations have all too frequently appealed to force as a means of self-protection. A church thus tends to become an end

Christianity and Social Process

rather than a means. It becomes concerned to maintain the political and economic *status quo*. Any change in existing conditions threatens its own well-being. It has repeatedly justified elements of the social order which, like slavery, are inconsistent with the ideals which the Christian movement professes.

Another reason for the failure of the Christian movement to enforce more thoroughly the values implicit in ideals derived from the teachings and life of Jesus, has been the predominant influence of the Old Testament in Christian teaching. The European society which, as has been pointed out, furnished patterns for Christian theologies, could easily grasp the idea of a Jehovah who led his armies to victory and punished his enemies and his rebellious subjects. So long as the entire Bible was held to be equally inspired and infallible, such a selective process was natural. If the Old Testament had been recognized as the record of the development of a religion within certain definite ethnic and geographical limits, it could not have been used as a collection of divine oracles. As it was, texts could easily be found in the Old

Moral Nature of the Christian Religion

Testament which give religious sanction to conquest and acts of retaliation. To the makers of theological systems such texts possessed the same authority as the idealism of prophets like Amos and Micah. The New Testament, being regarded as a completion of the divine program, was on no higher level than the Old. Jesus was regarded as having fulfilled prophecy, but his teachings would be interpreted in the light of Old Testament passages. His coming triumph was pictured by the early church in ways for which the practices of conquerors furnished the analogies. The portrayals of that conquest as found in the apocalyptic literature like the canonical Book of Revelation lack nothing of the brutality which was included in what the ancient world regarded as the laws of war. The Lamb of God became the lion of the tribe of Judah. He went forth to war in the spirit of King David.

The Old Testament continued to dominate the morals of the Protestant states. It gave to the Puritan his code of justice. The Protestant Confessions embody the Ten Commandments and generally the two great commands of love of God and love

Christianity and Social Process

for neighbor which Jesus declared were the chief commandments of the Old Testament. They even quote the new commandment by Jesus that his followers should love one another, but the application of such ideals was individual and private. Acquittal at the coming judgment was not in any way dependent upon morality; it was through faith and faith alone. Cromwell, after the terrible massacre his troops wrought at Drogheda, could write a letter to his daughter full of earnest admonition and direction for her religious life, but it contains no regret for the brutality of his soldiers. Massacre was justified by the Old Testament. There was no inconsistency between his massacre of the Irish and the command of Jehovah to massacre the Canaanites. It was not until the rise of the scientific study of the Bible that this authority of ancient Hebrew practices in the name of religion weakened. Perhaps the most influential element in the ethical advance of the Christian movement in modern times has been the historical study of the life and teachings of Jesus and the recognition of the Hebrew religion as the outcome of a process

Moral Nature of the Christian Religion

in which religious and moral ideals as well as agriculture and politics were outgrown or expanded.

v

From the beginnings of the Christian movement the Christian groups have demanded a higher morality on the part of their members than was practiced by others. They have believed they were obeying the Law of God. The early defenders of Christianity against charges of immorality and disloyalty to the Roman government emphasize this morality in detail. For it they were ready to face death itself. Even if their pictures of Christian virtues may be sometimes overdrawn, the actual contrast between the habits of the Christian communities and the *mores* of their pagan contemporaries must have been striking. An enemy like Celsus recognized what to him was the incomprehensible and incongruous heroism of even the humbler members of a Christian church. Christian communities have always been experimental laboratories in moral living. Sex has been brought within moral bounds, charity and honesty have been common. The failure of the early Christians

Christianity and Social Process

to realize any obligations to reform the social order naturally made them susceptible to ascetic practices, but even these served to keep alive the Christian's sense of values higher than self-indulgence or devotion to material goods.

The insistence that Christians are not to be "worldly" has always been maintained. The various sects have been especially rigorous in this regard. Some of them have organized codes of conduct that sharply distinguished their members from other persons, often extending such control to dress, food, and civic duties. Anabaptists, Mennonites, Puritans, Quakers are only a few of those Christian groups exemplifying that "sect" mind which Troeltsch regards as uncompromisingly opposed to any compromise with a double standard of morality. Less extreme Christian groups have uniformly emphasized morality among their members. A study of church records will show innumerable cases of discipline involving fornication, quarrelsomeness, dishonesty, and idleness. The socalled Blue Laws of Connecticut are now known to be forgeries, but there can be no question as to the moral standards of churches of early New Eng-

Moral Nature of the Christian Religion

land. If such church discipline was more negative than positive, opposed to normal pleasures, it none the less developed a conscientiousness that made life more capable of sacrifice and democracy. The Puritan is not popular today, but democracy is in large measure due to the power of self-direction he brought from his personal experience to political reconstruction.

In the codes of conduct which Christian groups have organized or adopted for themselves is one source of their influence upon social trends. The codes of any religion are valuable as attempts to direct conduct, and as more or less accurate gauges of the moral ideals of a religious group. In the nature of the case a code deals with matters about which a group is concerned. Not being able to foresee social trends, the code very properly undertakes to set forth what is regarded as involved in good social relations at the time when it is organized. Civilizations develop identical moral ideals as they reach the same stages of development. Theft, adultery, falsehood, are uniformly forbidden. Social life demands such prohibitions for its very existence. Yet the Ten Commandments, for example,

Christianity and Social Process

say nothing about the sin of slavery, and regard a wife as the property of her husband. In one of their forms there is a commandment not to boil a kid in its mother's milk. Such facts make it plain that a code conserves and even gives religious sanction to values already perceived in social life, but may fail to anticipate the moral tensions which will arise when the economic and political conditions under which it has been organized pass away. In consequence a moral and religious code, being a precipitate of group life or a social order, often becomes a hindrance to social progress. However efficient it may have been when organized it may tend to perpetuate outgrown institutions. It may even become so inapplicable to new conditions as to lead to its rejection, at the expense of the morality of the entire society.

Churches have been more than teachers; they have constituted social groups, in some cases believed to possess supernatural powers. Their social influence has been due largely to the fact that, in their offering divine salvation, they have undertaken to direct the moral behavior of their members. As has already been indicated, the re-

Moral Nature of the Christian Religion

sulting morality has been largely individualistic, although "mortal" sins may be said in general to be anti-social. In the Roman Church absolution could be gained, upon confession, for sins that were not mortal. In other churches divine forgiveness has been assured those who make a "general" confession and profess repentance. Such an adjustment of the moral life of individuals could hardly fail to be subject to abuse, but its influence in stabilizing *mores* is undeniable. There is an appreciable difference between the behavior of those who, both in Catholic and Protestant circles, undertake to embody the values of Christianity, and that of those who do not make such attempts. True, such differences are often superficial and do not extend beyond individual morals. Religious circles have sometimes insisted that differences between the Christians and the "world" include the avoidance of certain amusements. Undoubtedly, the prohibition of card-playing, dancing, and theater-going was grounded in a definite determination to avoid gambling and licentiousness, but it also implies a distrust of happiness. The Puritan, wherever found, has always feared uncontrolled enjoy-

Christianity and Social Process

ments and has endeavored to school himself to find happiness in so-called spirituality. It is no accident, therefore, that democracies should have first emerged in countries where such disciplined self-direction was inculcated.

The influence of the Christian group upon other groups presupposes the production of individuals who order their lives according to Christian principles. Through them a cross-fertilization has been established within a social order. Christian individuals both personally and collectively have brought some influence to bear upon groups to which they belong. The extent to which such transfer of discipline from one area to another is effective will always be a matter of dispute, but that it occurs must be admitted. By it motivation and ideals are transferred from one group to another.

VI

Beyond the moral education of its own members there is to be seen the direct influence exerted by the church upon contemporary practices. It is only necessary now to mention as illustrations the

Moral Nature of the Christian Religion

establishment of the observance of Sunday and various feast days by which labor was given leisure. These influences, however, have not always been thoroughly in accord with the idealistic aims of the Christian movement, and it would be impossible, therefore, to regard the betterment of social morality by the church as uniform. The principle of good-will finds different expressions in a feudal society than in a democracy. Men accustomed to coercion in their social relations see brutality in a different perspective from men by whom coercion itself is regarded as an evil. The expression of Christian ideals in a society that honors thrift would be different from that in a society that is communistic. An estimate of the moral significance of the Christian movement must, therefore, consider the *mores* and social attitudes of those who constitute the church.

VII

Here we meet a perplexing problem, that of the implementing of ideals as social behavior changes. That which would be socially advantageous for persons living in one climate and one

Christianity and Social Process

geographical milieu might not be at all advantageous for persons living in other conditions. The great moral teachers have been affected by social conditions, and their teachings have arisen from both the forms and the discontents of their own days. The laws of Manu could not have derived their form and application from the Hebrew history or the teaching of Jesus from a capitalistic civilization. It is therefore difficult to apportion the moral influence of the absolute idealist upon the community that adopts his teaching. In general, however, it will appear that the influence of the founder of a religion or the writer of a moral code is perpetuated in the values conserved by the movement he initiates. He sets the general direction in which the *mores* of his group of followers will develop. It is this general direction that establishes a broad line of difference between civilizations in which the personal equation of some teacher or teachers affects the complex of human activity and institutions in a social process. One has only to compare the structure of societies under the influence of the major religions to feel these differences. The teaching of Gautama as to

Moral Nature of the Christian Religion

love and peace is sublime, but the Buddhists of the Fujiwura period in Japan were fiercely military. So far as the Christian religion is concerned, the supreme ideal is the personality of Jesus, his devotion to the welfare of others, his refusal to enforce ideals in ways that would cause pain or suffering to others, and his complete repudiation of the spirit of acquisitiveness. Whether or not the teaching of Jesus was an interim ethics intended for a social order that was presently to come to a catastrophic end makes little difference in the actual influence exerted by the religious movement centered about him. The Christian community has accepted his words as the final formulas of moral idealism, yet, paradoxically, only in sporadic cases have Christian groups undertaken to put them into effect. The pressure of human nature and social practices has been too great. The human stock that gave rise to Western civilization was far enough from being gentle or non-acquisitive. Its natural bent for cruelty and oppression was furthered by the misconceptions of the religion forced upon them by conquerors and rulers. The establishment of Christian celibate groups also

Christianity and Social Process

had a biological influence upon Western civilization. The more forceful qualities of the human stock became dominant. What else could be expected when for centuries men and women of spiritual qualities had no children?

Yet it would be incorrect to say that the Christian ideals of love and sacrifice have had no influence and that the history of the Christian movement is that of a disloyalty to its founder and a continuous hypocrisy. The inconsistency between the practices of Christians and their profession of faith in the divine Saviour can be understood as one brings to the investigation some knowledge of social psychology. The influence of one group upon another, of one social institution upon others, is gradual. Absolute ideals have pervasive influence especially in times of economic discontent. Most great social movements have centered about undefined abstract terms: liberty, equality, fraternity, justice, brotherhood, salvation. These are potent almost in the same proportion as they are left in the region of appeal. Only when men attempt to embody them in social behavior may they become

Moral Nature of the Christian Religion

sources of dissension and be compromised by programs.

Finally, the distinction between attitudes and the techniques enables us to understand the relation of Christian morality to social trends. We must distinguish between the basic values of the movement and the techniques furnished by contemporary culture by which they were expressed. Such historical-mindedness should not blunt our minds to the fact that when once human beings undertake to act in accordance with what is shocking to their intelligence or to their moral sense, their attitude is to be condemned. To plead ignorance of the proper way of procedure may explain, but not necessarily justify, an act that injures others. For the ignorance itself may be the result of moral indifference. There are altogether too many instances, both in the past and in the present, where men have perverted their moral attitude by a persistent rejection of intelligent action warranted to benefit others. Opposition to laws compelling doctors to drop nitrate of silver into the eyes of new-born babies, or to benefit the conditions of women wage-earners, or to permit instruction in birth control, has been due to organized religious influence. This opposition has been conscientiously urged, but sincerity is not necessarily a test of wisdom. Christians who refuse to adopt techniques shown by scientific experts to be capable of furthering human welfare are not only unintelligent but morally inconsistent. No matter how beautiful the architect's drawing, a marble house cannot be built out of mud bricks. The use of good techniques implies good intentions. Good intentions imply good individuals. And good persons should have good sense. The struggle for the appropriation of more effective techniques is one of long standing, but advance is apparent. In medieval Europe an experimental scientist was regarded by the clergy, if not by people generally, as having sold himself to the devil. The conflict between theology and science has continued to our own day, yet scientific discoveries accepted as trustworthy are now being built into Christian teaching by individuals or by modernist minorities. Christian bodies in developing social service have not hesitated to adopt the most scientific instruments and methods in hospitals. Increasingly the methods of

Moral Nature of the Christian Religion

the sociologist are also being appropriated by church workers. All such appropriations of techniques by the Christian movement indicate new adjustment with a social process. Ideals are being more intelligently implemented.

VIII

The problems of Christian behavior, difficult as they are in a civilization in which the present Christian religion has developed, become increasingly complicated when a civilization in its economic, financial, military, as well as scientific aspects, is appropriated by a civilization which has already its religious sanctions. If human history be viewed in the large, it would seem to be an evident conclusion that the basic values of a religion will not become operative in morality except as they work through the institutions and customs of a civilization. In the process of interracial and intercultural contacts this fact has been repeatedly overlooked. Just as the early Christians of Jerusalem thought at first it was necessary that the non-Jewish professors of the Christian faith should take over the customs of the original Christian group, so it has

Christianity and Social Process

happened repeatedly in missionary operations that it has been felt that the institutions and theologies of western civilization were indispensable for those who in other civilizations accepted the Christian faith. But I can see no reason to doubt that Christianity in civilizations which are taking over the Western ideas and techniques will repeat its own history. Just as the Christian movement appropriated many of the elements of the Hellenistic civilization, will the Christian movement in the civilizations of Asia be organized by the utilization of such permanent institutions, customs, and ideas as are capable of being directed by the Christian estimate of the worth of the individual, and of his relations with God. The process by which these new types of Christian religion may be developed will undoubtedly be slow, but we can already see that it is under way. The same Christian ferment is present as in Western civilization. There will be evolved from the social process *mores* and institutions capable of carrying forward this basic idea of the value of the human individual as he grows more personal because of a faith in the presence of a Heavenly Father. I look forward,

Moral Nature of the Christian Religion

therefore, to still further differentiation of the Christian movement. The implementing of Christian idealism in institutions, modes of thought and behavior will be determined by the elements of the respective civilizations themselves.

IV

CHRISTIANITY AND THE INDIVIDUAL

THE influence of the Christian movement upon other elements of Western civilization, like that of every other group is to be seen in the extent to which its members have coöperated to fulfill the function of the group itself. It is one thing to organize ideals and quite another to test their practicability in actual life. The function of a Christian group is to socialize the values involved in its formation. The degree of success with which it is able by actual behavior to incorporate these values in life will be the measure of its efficiency. It is true that the worth of this influence may be tested by philosophers, but the supreme test will be seen in the part it has played in human relations. Among those values which the Christian movement has embodied, none possesses larger

Christianity and the Individual

significance than that the individual has personal worth—something more than that of a peripatetic chemical laboratory driven by the sex instinct. With this characteristic Christianity challenges many of the findings of biologists and certain groups of psychologists. Its insistence upon the worth of the individual also runs counter to those social movements which magnify class solidarity.

It has become fashionable to sneer at individualism, and its child democracy. In many countries on the continent of Europe the hope of reaching the better social order by way of democracy has been deadened by the monoxide of inexperienced democrats' loquacity. Communism, with its reliance upon mass coercion, is consistent in its antagonism to Christianity. This distrust of the worth of the individual, born of social theory, is supplemented by the tendency of psychologists to center attention upon those characteristics of the human personality which are shared by animals. But true understanding of human personality will not be gained by centering investigation upon its sub-personal elements. If there is nothing in human life but the capacity to reënact physical inheritances there is

Christianity and Social Process

little hope for us at the present juncture. One can understand why the cult of pessimism and futility can be so popular among those who do not believe in the personal worth of individuals. No other attitude is permitted those who find in the human individual nothing more self-directing than qualms of perturbed viscera and the inhibitions of enlarged glands. Why should there be any more regard for an animal that walks on two legs than for one that walks on four legs?

I

Christian dogma has not been built upon myopic optimism. Theologians have distrusted human nature since Adam. Every person has been held to be not only unfortunate, but doomed to suffer from the wrath of God. From the time of Augustine, as Browning has said,

> Christianity has dared point its dart at the head of a lie,
> Taught original sin, the corruption of man's heart.

Theological thought among liberal Protestants

Christianity and the Individual

has tended to overlook this pessimism, but it is being forced by current psychology to recognize facts which Augustine in a pre-scientific age explained in political patterns. To abandon a doctrine of original sin is not to deny the elements of the human personality which led to its formulation.

But the Christian movement has held that human individuals can be saved. The distrust of human nature apart from proper relations with God has been offset by the belief that the individual can be regenerated by God and can gain the supreme good of immortal happiness. The Christian movement is built around this confidence in the salvation of the human individual. From its very inception it has treated the worth of the human individual as not limited by his animal survivals or by death.

It is inevitable that morals should be affected by views as to post-mortem existence. Such a belief has played an obvious part in the social behavior of Hindus and followers of certain other religions, and the morals of the Christian movement have been both directly and indirectly shaped

Christianity and Social Process

by conceptions of conduct which would be consistent with the individual's relationship with a saving God. It would be difficult to say just how far such behavior is at present conditioned within Western civilization by fear of hell or hope of heaven, but certainly the moral teaching which has been wrought into social practices has come from those to whom the supreme worth of the human individual was to be seen in a future life.

In Western civilization morality developed under the general belief that human nature has more survival value than that of other animals, and this morality continues to a greater or less extent in the customs which a social group preserves. Those individuals of scientific temperament who, like Huxley, disbelieve in personal immortality, indignantly deny the danger that such an attitude implies moral deterioration. But while in any highly organized society a denial of personal immortality would not introduce an orgy of animalism, it can hardly be questioned that such an evaluation of the human personality would set up a new scale of moral values. It would be difficult to understand the ethics of religions like Moham-

Christianity and the Individual

medanism, Christianity, and Hinduism without recognizing the part which future rewards and punishments have played in human behavior. While there have been moral systems developed without reference to God, there have been no ethnic or national *mores* based on the presumption that human personality becomes extinct with death. The precise nature of the future life is of less importance than the fact that the behavior of men and women has been held to have a direct bearing upon their fortunes after death. Whether the philosophy be that of Karma or of heaven and hell, such beliefs have given sanction to moral codes.

In the words of the "Laws of Manu"[1]:

> In the next world neither father nor mother are there
> As helpers; nor son, wife or kinsman.
> His virtue alone is there.
> Each creature is born alone; dies alone;
> Alone enjoys his good deeds,
> Alone his bad deeds.
> Leaving his dead body on the ground,
> His kinsmen go away with averted faces.
> His virtue follows him.

(4:238-242)   [1] Burnett and Hopkins, *Ordinances* of *Manu*, quoted in Hume, *Treasure House* of *Living Religions*, 67.

Christianity and Social Process

> Virtue will swiftly carry up to the other world
> A man of dominant virtue
> Who has extinguished his sin.

This concentration upon the salvation of the individual from Satan, sin, and death, in large measure explains why the early Christians had no thought of establishing a new social order and no interest in social reform. Their morality was strictly individual. Their kingdom was not of this world. Roman police would have checked any reform movement, even if it had entered the minds of Roman citizens. Until the divinely established reign of Christ came, the Christian individual was to be charitable, kindly, and obedient to the law. Christians did not withdraw from the affairs of social life, but went about conscious of being citizens of this new kingdom which was to come. The full development of their new individuality would be reached by the resurrection of the body, an expression which was not precisely defined, except that Paul would say it was to be spiritual rather than of the flesh. The ideal of this complete individuality was, so to speak, dramatized in the conception of Christ, who exemplified not only

Christianity and the Individual

virtues which the Christian individual was to possess, but also the triumph of that new individuality over death.

Such appeals to the desire for future well being have been condemned as appeals to selfishness. To save one's soul is regarded by critics of the Christian religion as unworthy of high-minded persons. But such criticism is not altogether just. It must be admitted that popular preaching, particularly of the past, has abounded in crude appeals to future rewards and punishments. If theological pictures of heaven and hell were to be taken literally, Christianity would properly make no appeal to intelligently religious persons. If, however, they are regarded as homiletic devices to stimulate desire for the real goal of human hopes and a keener appreciation of the worth of the individual, they are less objectionable.

II

As a general religious movement Christianity does not aim at an atomistic individuality. It undertakes to increase the individual's personal value by making him social. It thus makes the law of

Christianity and Social Process

coördination, which operates throughout nature, in the case of human individuals appear as love. From the viewpoint of sociology a person is a socialized individual. Christianity is thus justified in insisting upon the social attitude of love rather than the egoistic attitude of acquisitiveness as essential in the development of the ideal individual. Here again the significance of the life of Jesus as a dramatization of his teachings has been of utmost value. "While we were yet sinners," says the apostle, "Christ died for us." If men are to be children of the Heavenly Father according to the teaching of Jesus, they must love their enemies, pray for those that despitefully use them, and bless those that curse them.

The Christian conception of the worth of the socialized individual is obviously not to be identified with various current philosophies of self-realization and self-expression. In them the element of service to others is not emphasized. The immediate aim is self-centered pleasure.

True, well-being has an emotional accompaniment; but it is one thing to seek emotional experience and another thing to develop a normal life

Christianity and the Individual

that will induce happiness. It is the universal teaching of philosophers that the search for pleasure is always disappointing and ultimately debilitating, but that the pursuit of virtue, or, as the Christian religion would say, the attainment of a moral salvation through the grace of God is a source of peace and joy. As Sakyamuni said, "Happiness is the bloom upon virtue." Happiness is the outcome of perfection. Man is not perfect because he is happy, but happy because he is perfect. And he is to be perfect as God is perfect; that is, dominated by love.

Throughout its history the Christian movement has preserved this concept of perfection of personality as sacrificial social-mindedness finding expression in service to others. The methods of rendering that service have been furnished by contemporary civilizations and have sometimes been unintelligent. To many earnest souls separation from social life has seemed the only condition which the saved individual could approve. Thousands of Christians have been ascetic. They have sought the salvation of their souls by withdrawal from the social order as far as humanly possible.

Christianity and Social Process

Yet such withdrawal could seldom be complete. What is more, it is contrary to the supreme values embodied in the Christian movement. In the various reforms which have marked the history of the Christian church monasticism has been repeatedly condemned as a means of attaining salvation. At the same time, many monastic orders have nobly obeyed the command Jesus laid upon his disciples that they should not seek honor but service. In this they have been loyal to a central value in the Christian movement.

III

The Christian religion as a social behavior has always been that of men subject to many social forces. Within these forces the Christian ideal of the worth of the individual has worked as a moral ferment. Its influence, however, has been only slowly felt in the social process of the West. The evolution of Western society has been largely determined by a succession of conquests. The presence of a conquered group has served to prevent the recognition of the worth of individuals as such. It is easier to promise equality in heaven than to

Christianity and the Individual

free slaves and serfs. The historical process from which Western civilization has emerged has hindered the full application to human life of the Christian ideals of personal worth. It would be gratifying for a member of the Christian community to discover that the Christian church has stood steadily for an increase in the personal rights of the individual, but unfortunately any such statement is subject to serious modifications. Christians have not escaped current social conditions. Yet the influence of the ideal has been felt in different degrees. Within the church of the Middle Ages an individual might move out of the class in which he had been born and acquire distinction in church and state, even becoming pope. But outside of its own circles ecclesiastical policy did not attempt to break down social barriers. While it somewhat modified chivalry by emphasizing the duties of the strong to the weak, the church did not oppose the social stratification set by feudalism. It is to the discredit of the French church that at the time of the outbreak of the Revolution it held serfs. Yet Councils repeatedly passed laws against the slave-trade, the enslavement of Christians, and encour-

Christianity and Social Process

aged the manumission of slaves. Social evolution does not proceed uniformly, and when new economic conditions and classes emerge there have always been those who attempted to exploit them in their own interest. The church for centuries accepted slavery as a social fact, but its values were against it. The history of all social orders forbids the expectation that social barriers and strata can be instantaneously abolished except by revolution, and revolutions are extremely expensive. In Western civilization there has never been ritual classification of society, and in consequence the application of ideals to new social conditions has not been hindered by inherited religious systems of castes. But it can hardly be said that the abolition of the stratified society of mediæval Europe, with its privileged and unprivileged, its orders and nobilities, was due solely to the influence of the church. As organized bodies of socially privileged clerics, certain churches have opposed many a social movement extending personal privileges at the expense of the *status quo*. In so doing such Christian groups disregarded the basic principles of the movement inaugurated by Jesus. They have stood for the

Christianity and the Individual

maintenance of rights rather than for the democratizing of privileges.

It is not difficult to see that Christian ideals have not always been intelligently administered. When an ideal is translated into action, it becomes subject to a social situation. That which might be regarded as moral under one set of conditions might be condemned under another as willful selfishness. The techniques of love have usually been derived from the social order in which service has been rendered. The morally sincere Christian may thus become confused as to just what course of action should be taken. Particularly has this been true of both Catholic and early Protestant theories of the relation of church and state. Luther no more than his contemporaries championed absolute religious liberty. Ecclesiastical differences were allied with political interests.

Yet subject as men have been to the pressure of social conditions, there has been, at least in the last five centuries in Western civilization, a tendency to recognize the worth of the individual as a person and to develop his personal worth by stimulating him to service of others. Behind this moral motivation has lain the Christian conception of God and faith in Jesus as the revealer of love as a divine attribute. The cross has often been a magical symbol, but it symbolizes the meaning of the mind of Christ which Christians have been urged to possess. The monastic life, especially of the early Franciscans, was supposed to be modeled after that of Jesus. Thomas Aquinas as an ethical teacher was individualist to the extent of all but neglecting the social order. To him the reign of God is internal justice and peace and spiritual joy. Indeed, to the schoolmen the ideal character in so far as it was monastic was intensely individual. The same is true of the mystics like Hugo and St. Victor. The individual was to seek his own ecstatic experiences of God through meditation, prayer, and the Eucharist. To Innocent III, among other teachers, the world was an evil to be contemned as evil, and the way of salvation was the individual's withdrawal from social relations.

Emphasis upon egoistic individualism must in large measure account for the rôle played by the church as an institution. Its persistent challenge to the oppression to which a feudal society subjected

Christianity and the Individual

the unprivileged, was never extended by the medieval teachers to economic and political relations. They, like the church, accepted the social order as divinely established. It was not until that social order yielded to forces within itself that the individual was seen to have more than other-worldly worth.

The Christian movement was a ferment in the social readjustments of the sixteenth and seventeenth centuries. Despite the intolerance of newly formed state churches Protestantism marked the beginning of a new stage in the estimate of the individual. The laity now had the approach to God which had been restricted to the clergy. The bearing of this upon political life was, it is true, not immediate, but a new feeling of freedom was engendered. It was exclusively in Protestant states that democracy was born.

IV

The social movement known as democracy illustrates how the Christian has responded to and affected social process. It would be inaccurate to say that democratic individualism was the outcome of

Christianity and Social Process

the Christian movement alone. In no small degree it was due to changes in the economic life in portions of Europe and on the frontier in America. Ecclesiastical organizations have been all too frequently champions of an existing social order, and they have repeatedly opposed efforts at democratizing social and political privileges. How tragic may be the outcome of the failure to perceive that the equalities of heaven should be anticipated on earth can be seen in the fate of the Christian church of Russia. The Russian church was all but oblivious to new developments in economic and political processes. Indeed, it was openly the champion of social conditions which checked the development of the personal rights of individuals. Protestant Christians have been especially adventurous in their insistence upon the general worth of the individual as one capable not only of participation in the coming Kingdom of God, but in town meetings and legislatures. Such recognition of the rights of the individual did not come from the philosophy of Rousseau, with his impossible assumption of an ideal but lost "state of nature," or from any other philosophy. It can be

Christianity and the Individual

traced back to the constitutional development of England. There independency, with its recognition of the rights of individuals, gained influence because of the struggles of Puritans and High Church parties. Freedom of conscience was urged by John Milton in opposition to enforced religious conformity. The churches of the American Colonies were here pioneers. The conditions in which they were placed, their organization by the middle class of England, their growth in self-government, all tended to develop a sense of the worth of the individual. Roger Williams gave his little Colony of Rhode Island a constitution separating church and state and granting absolute religious freedom. The Declarations of the Rights of Man which figured so largely in the democratic movements of the eighteenth century have been shown to be descendants of formulas that the New England Colonies had heard from their religious leaders.

For our present consideration the question whether democracy is due solely to Christianity is not so important as the fact that the Christian conception of the supreme worth of the individual rather than of a class is now seriously endangered

Christianity and Social Process

by social programs that make class struggle a means to class supremacy, or seek to prevent the passage of individuals from one economic group to another. It is thoroughly consistent for the first of these social programs to oppose Christianity and for the second to make the church subservient to the state. As the social tensions of the eighteenth century gave rise to such Christian movements as those of Wesley and the Baptists, so this new tension demands that the Christian movement be concerned with the rights of the individual as a member of some economic or political group.

v

The most elemental form in which individual needs have been regarded as involving social obligations by the Christian movement is the duty of charity. Wherever the Christian community has moved there has been emphasis laid upon the Christian's responsibility to contribute aid to others. The limitation to fellow Christians of such aid has long since passed, and charity has grown both scientific, as in the Red Cross and hundreds of charitable organizations, and worldwide in its

Christianity and the Individual

sweep. I do not mean to say that charity is limited to Christians, or is an exclusive Christian virtue. What I would point out is that the Christian moral impulse of service to others has found expression in charity. Whenever there is human need, whether it be in one's own nation or in other nations, a civilization under Christian influence has consecrated the modern genius for organization to the relief of such need. Without a sense of the worth of the individual, such generosity would hardly be practiced except as a superstitious desire to derive from almsgiving merit which will assure blessings after death.

What is true of charity is true of other efforts to ameliorate the evils of our social life. Even among those indifferent to the church there is a dedication of modern techniques to Christian values. Whatever divergent theological beliefs intelligent citizens may hold, they agree in professing that genuine religion and state action must regard human well-being. Children are cared for, widows are pensioned, hospitals are established, unemployment must be relieved and if possible ended. The chief difficulty in carrying such convictions into action is the hesitation men naturally feel to share their own privileges with others. Without religious motives such sacrifice is seldom accomplished without coercion. The socialization of privilege by intelligent technique will be directly furthered by a sense of the worth of personality. And this is increasingly a characteristic of a social process in which Christianity shares.

VI

The Christian movement has not always been sufficiently intelligent to draw from love its corollary of equality. As a result largely of economic forces, the modern world is facing a series of changes of the utmost importance. Perhaps the most difficult of all tasks set the modern world is the establishment of a morality among individuals who are equals but who are increasingly organized in economic groups.

Here the world is almost without precedent. The progressive members of every religion are forced to combat inherited belief in divine sanction for social stratification with consequent different moral obligations. The Christian movement shared

Christianity and the Individual

in a feudal or militaristic society where the prevailing virtues were those of courage and obedience. The value of an act in such a social order varied according to the social status of the class to which the actor belonged. This would be particularly true in the case of injuries to a person. In such societies the superior has rights over those dependent on him, but those dependents have not the same rights over their lord. The same was true in the development of the absolute monarchies of the sixteenth and seventeenth centuries in Europe. There the church became an aspect of society which recognized inequalities between ruler and the ruled as divinely established, and naturally insisted upon those virtues which such a relationship involved. Even Luther taught that "political and economical ordinances are divine, because God Himself ordained them as He did the moon and other creatures." Such conceptions extended into theology, and we have the idea of God as absolute sovereign who punished and saved according to His own good pleasure. Over against him humanity had no rights.

But Western civilization outgrew such conserv-

Christianity and Social Process

atism. Cartwright led in democratizing the church by insisting that ministers are all equal and should be chosen by their congregations. Once chosen, however, they were not to be removed except for open sin or heresy. Calvinism preserved these conceptions of the church and brought them to bear upon the organization of states, though without denying the duty of the state to punish heretics. Independency in England was really based on the freedom of the individual in religion.

From the eighteenth century the destruction of the feudal type of society by the rise of the commercial or middle class, now commonly known as the *bourgeoisie*, is evident. In England, the United States, and France there has emerged a conception of the state which made individualism dominant and made the government a sort of executive committee of the people. Sovereignty lies in the people rather than in some family.

Political equality, however, was at the start established between men, but not with women nor with men and women. Until the last fifty years a woman, both in Europe and in America, lacked many of the rights which the man possessed, both

Christianity and the Individual

political and economic. The church gave sanction to this inequality on the basis of the Pauline teaching as to the distinction between men and women seen within the Græco-Roman world. Because of a variety of reasons, chiefly, doubtless, that of the development of education of women and their achievement of economic status in society, this inequality of rights between men and women is being rapidly removed. Most of the new states which have been shaped since the World War have recognized women not as weaker vessels, but as persons possessed of economic and political rights as well as men. In older democracies such as those of Great Britain and the United States, similar changes have taken place.

The apologist for Christianity is accustomed to credit it with the improvement of the situation of women. Such credit is not unwarranted, but it can hardly be exclusive. Many forces combined to establish the present status of women as persons in Western civilization. It is, however, noteworthy that in the very first stages of its development Christianity took sex into the field of morals. Chastity was demanded of members of the Christian community on the ground that the body is the temple of the Holy Spirit. And as the institutions of the Christian movement became more sharply developed, this new moral ideal was increasingly apparent. The early Christian apologists constantly referred to the purity of life which their religion enforced. It would be difficult to discover a sharper contrast than that between their words and the conceptions of the relations of sexes as set forth in moralists like Plutarch and the practices which were countenanced in the worship of certain gods and goddesses. The final form of this conception of women as potential persons is to be found in the statement of Paul that in Christ there is neither male nor female.

In actual practice, however, the Christian movement for many years was so much a phase of social life as to fail to introduce fully this idealism. From the days of Augustine sex was held by theologians to be an evidence of the original sin and corrupt nature which humanity derived from Adam. Celibacy, which came from the non-Hebraic pagan countries and religions despite the evils with which it was accompanied, was regarded as

Christianity and the Individual

more spiritual than the marriage state, and monasteries and nunneries were for hundreds of years a testimony to the desire for holiness which the church taught could be possible only for the unmarried. In our own day the Catholic church and the more conservative elements of Protestantism are opposed to any radical change in the position of married women as proposed by advocates of birth control.

So far as evidence with which I am acquainted is concerned, there is no ground for believing that the honor paid Mary served to elevate the status of women or give dignity to marriage. Indeed, the logical implication of her virginity was to subordinate marriage. The mediæval church was not much concerned about increasing the rights of women beyond those which would be set by their status as mothers. Only in the case of abbesses and occasional sovereigns did women reach preëminence. The women saints of the Middle Ages were, practically without exception, unmarried.

This treatment of women as personally inferior to men was an aspect of a now outgrown social order in the West. The influence of Teutonic and

Christianity and Social Process

Roman matrimonial laws forbade economic independence on the part of women. By the very structure of society women were dependent upon men for support. It is too much to expect that men living in a feudal or other type of military society should anticipate the individualistic development of the industrial age, but the influence of the church guaranteed women such rights as accepted institutions permitted. Facing a social order born of violence, the church became the protector of women. It maintained the family as a permanent institution, attacked sexual irregularities, and by treating marriage as a sacrament lessened the proprietary rights of a husband in his wife, and at least laid the foundation for a monogamy in which the woman as well as the man had personal rights. It insisted upon the wife's claim to her dower and her right to make a will. That women in the Christian lands have been given freedom of action, have not been veiled or secluded in the homes of their husbands, but have shared in social life, is due to many causes, but the Christian movement did not in the name of religion undertake to reduce such privileges. Schools and colleges at first restricted to

Christianity and the Individual

men gradually opened to women. Most of the women's colleges were in fact founded by Christian groups. The first women's college in England, for example, was largely due to the influence of Frederic Denison Maurice, and in the United States practically every such college was the child of the church.

The same can be said of the early efforts to pass legislation preventing prostitution, and suppressing the white-slave traffic. The concern of Western civilization regarding such evils has been due in large measure to Christian influences.

To the student of society and morals this emergence of at least theoretical personal equality of both men and women appears as one of the most momentous in history. It is true that such equality has not been fully attained and that social control in many lands perpetuates inequalities born of past conditions. But the events of the last fifteen or twenty years show a distinct trend in the direction of such equality.

Both in domestic and in economic life, this trend has weakened the old authority which was derived from the social order. The Christian church as the

Christianity and Social Process

representative of moral idealism and the progressively increased personal value of the individual, finds itself confronted with a perplexing question. The old techniques which it used in a society marked by social inequality do not operate in a society that recognizes the equality of persons—where the husband no longer has legal authority over his wife, and parents no longer have unlimited control of their children; where the family is no longer under the control of the church, divorce is an affair of the courts, and the relations of the sexes are approached from biology rather than morality.

These trends in Western civilization are furthered by new economic groups indifferent to religion and distrustful of unregimented competition. If the Christian movement is to fulfill its function it must not camouflage cowardly avoidance of its social responsibility under calls to worship and mystical experiences. It must regard intelligent morality as the true channel of divine help. It must realize that its failure to adjust its moral education to new situations is one cause of the inefficiencies of democracy. Individuals if

Christianity and the Individual

equally of worth must be made more personal by being made more social. A dictator can develop efficiency much more promptly than can a democracy, but a dictatorship that begins with efficiency is very apt to end in a tyranny that suppresses individual initiative and freedom. The church as a social institution can be of exceptional service to a social order by raising up individuals who are possessed of that moral self-direction which a social order demands. In its moral education the church must recognize the social relations in which individuals live. The centering of attention upon the traits of character which disregard such relations results too often, as experience has shown, in monasticism or non-participation in social life. An individual lacking a sense of responsibility for a social order is apt to be an exploiter of that order. The church in its emphasis upon honesty and chastity has helped produce individuals capable of recognizing group relations in business and the family, but it needs to inculcate still greater appreciation of other virtues. In moments of tension like the present, the extension of altruism to the dynamic aspects of the

Christianity and Social Process

social process which lie in group relations is the responsibility of the church. So-called character education and formal courses in ethics in schools cannot displace the influence of a social group like the church. For in the midst of a developing recognition of human equality it can supply motives for the socialization of the individual which no other agency possesses.

V

CHRISTIANITY AND THE MORALITY OF GROUPS

CHRISTIANITY as a form of social behavior does not presuppose atomistic individualism. As a phase of Western civilization it has affected and been affected by groups. Every society, from the most primitive to the most complicated, consists of groups organized for certain definite ends. Through them individuals are able coöperatively to accomplish that which would have been otherwise impossible. In some civilizations these groups are dependent upon birth, and are mutually exclusive castes. In most cases they serve economic or political interests. The integrity and continuance of a group are always matters of first concern, since recognized privileges are attached to membership in it. The feudal classes, the distinction between owners and slaves, the various caste systems of the world, the economic structure of modern society, are illustrations of how a social order has developed as those possessed of common interests have coöperated in groups. The history of many peoples shows how difficult it is to modify the resulting social structure. Especially is this true when social practices are consolidated and made a part of religion. In such cases any disregard of the *mores* of a group is likely to injure an individual. Social ostracism, loss of property, the breaking of family ties, are among the penalties which such disregard entails. The relation of persons to each other, in fact, is seldom direct. Individuals cannot be detached from groups and groups themselves stand in relationship to each other.

I

At the present time the individual is in danger of being submerged in group solidarity. Communism, fascism, state nationalism, reorganized democracy are putting an end to that individualism from which the democracy of the eighteenth and

Christianity and the Morality of Groups

nineteenth centuries sprang. The relationship of groups to one another is of primary concern for the organization of a morality adapted to new phases of Western civilization. Such a morality must touch the relationship of individuals within a group not only to each other, but also to the individuals of other groups. Can one act as if there were no group interests? And this leads to the still more difficult question as to whether there can be any morality in the case of larger groups, such as economic classes and nations. Even small groups which, as in the case of families, seem to have reached permanence, are now being disintegrated through the influence of new social conditions. The relations of individuals and their standards of conduct are affected by the control of the groups to which they belong. Loyalty is even erected into a philosophy. The exploiting of economic groups by so-called racketeers is clearly a social menace, but moral codes which will define the relations of organizations of wage-earners to those of employers, and of the state to both, are still largely tentative.

In a social order marked by castes or classes,

Christianity and Social Process

membership in one group is conditioned by membership in another. In a democracy membership in one group is, at least theoretically, not conditioned by membership in another; that is to say, individuals are free to belong to such religious, cultural, and economic groups as they may choose. In actual practice, however, such freedom of choice is by no means perfect. Groups whose interests are opposed do not countenance the participation of their members in other groups judged antagonistic. Group conflict, in consequence, increasingly marks Western civilization.

II

Ideally, the Christian principle of love—that is to say, of coöperation and coördination on a personal level—should be as true of groups as of individuals. As a matter of fact such a situation has seldom existed. Christians have usually recognized the relations set by their social order, but the idealism of the Christian movement is difficult to express in group conduct. There have been those who thought that the only way of applying the principles of love to human life is for individuals

Christianity and the Morality of Groups

to withdraw from social relations. Such a technique of escape, however, has never been successful in avoiding social obligations. For out of it have emerged organizations in which the problems of the relations of individuals to a group and of the group to the state have reappeared. Still other Christians have obeyed the teachings of Jesus as to non-resistance by recourse to absolute pacifism; but even pacifists are affected, indirectly if not directly, by the economic conditions set up by war. A few Protestant sects have refused to assume civic as well as military duties, but they have found it impossible to avoid contact with those who recognize the obligations of citizenship.

There has been a tendency among some Christian bodies as well as monastic fraternities to distinguish between the morals of the individual and the morals of social action. As a result, such bodies center attention upon salvation after death and refuse to consider themselves obligated to deal with economic, political, and racial issues. But to abstract the relations of an individual belonging to a group from the relations of that group is all but impossible. No such distinction exists in actual life.

Christianity and Social Process

Even in minor matters the individual is influenced by membership in his group. A married person cannot act as if unmarried; a member of a trade union cannot bargain independently; an individual may be kind and charitable, yet as a member of some economic group he may be a relentless competitor and an unscrupulous lawbreaker. There is, indeed, an ever-present danger of schism in character because of which a person would justify, in the case of a group, action which he would condemn in the case of an individual as injurious to human welfare. And such a schism will continue until moral ideals are developed in the relationships of groups themselves.

The Christian movement as a whole has never attempted to escape from group obligations which citizenship has entailed. Christians have paid taxes, shared in the organization of laws, and despite a few exceptions have recognized the right of the state to enforce, under threat of punishment, observance of its laws.

Indeed, as humanity is now constituted, a social order in which there was no recourse to coercion seems impossible. Whether coercion be that of

Christianity and the Morality of Groups

police power, or of non-participation like that of the followers of Gandhi, does not affect the principle at stake. The moral quality of the technique varies, but the determination to force others to do something against their will is the same. But how else can a group control an opposing minority?

III

A group is functional. It exists not for its own self, but to aid its constituent individuals in the satisfaction of their desires. Even if it disappeared, the individuals would still exist. A social group is a creation of its own members. Any consideration of the moral relations of groups must, therefore, take into account the welfare of the individuals as it is affected by the purpose for which the group was formed. The neglect of this elemental fact has been the source of incalculable misery. The church, the nation, the economic guild, the social class, have all been treated as ends. Almost in the same proportion as they have been highly organized has their functional value been obscured in their refusal to adopt methods consistent with their ideal purposes. One tragic illustration of this is the

Christianity and Social Process

recourse to persecution on the part of religious organizations devoted professedly to the ideals of Jesus. To maintain their integrity seemed more imperative than the choice of a method in accord with their ideals. Indeed, we have only too much evidence that religious groupings may be sources of evil as well as of good. The history of western Europe is full of violence and wars sanctified by the Christian church if not by the consciences of Christians. Influential as were the Crusades in awakening western Europe from feudalism, they brought Christians to the support of un-Christian behavior. The so-called Wars of Religion and the Thirty Years' War are instances of the terrible brutality that follows the identification of religious loyalties with political rivalries.

The papacy has repeatedly claimed control over governments. The secret of its power lay not merely in the enormous wealth which the church accumulated during the feudal period, but ultimately in its claim to supernatural status. The power of binding and loosing which the church claimed was derived from Christ himself gave force to its excommunication. A person or a politi-

Christianity and the Morality of Groups

cal unit that came under the ban of the church was outside of all loyalties on earth and salvation after death. In a state where the bull of excommunication was recognized, marriages and burials could not be properly solemnized and the inhabitants were bereft of means of grace and freed from allegiance to their rulers. Henry IV of Germany humbled himself before Gregory VII at Canossa in order to have the ban of excommunication lifted before he could successfully struggle with the German nobles. Innocent III compelled John of England to admit that he held his kingdom as a fief from the pope. Popes deposed kings as heretics, and in some cases incited neighboring monarchs to seize the heretic's kingdom. Elizabeth of England was excommunicated and her subjects freed from allegiance, and Philip II was supported in his attack upon England. In 1493 Alexander VI, acting on the basis of the "plenitude of our apostolic power," made over to the kings of Spain and Portugal all the islands and continents of North and South America west and south of a line drawn from the North Pole to the South Pole one hundred leagues west and south of the Azores and

Christianity and Social Process

Cape De Verde Islands, except such territory as was in the actual possession of some other Christian king or prince on December 25, 1492.

Nor was this reliance upon coercion limited to the field where religion and politics overlapped. The belief that the church furnished the only means by which members of a lost race could share in the divine mercy was held to justify the use of force to prevent the weakening of the church through heresies. With the eleventh century persecution of heretics assumed cruel proportions. The papal legate declared that 20,000 persons were killed in the crusade against the Albigenses. In the middle of the thirteenth century the Inquisition was established for the purpose of exterminating heresy by confiscation of property, torture, and death. The last-named penalty was justified even by so great a soul as Thomas Aquinas. The horrors of the Inquisition in Spanish territory are well known. The attempt of Philip II to crush out heresy in the Netherlands has been estimated to have resulted in the death of at least 25,000, but prior to his time 50,000 persons were executed for their religious beliefs between 1522 and

Christianity and the Morality of Groups

1556. The recent anti-clericalism in Spain can be best understood in view of the fact that in 1851 a concordat was made by Isabella and Pius IX according to which all religious cults except Catholicism were forbidden in Spain and all education was under the direction of the church. In persecution the church relied usually upon political authority, over which it exerted an inescapable influence.

This reliance of Catholic Christianity upon coercive methods can be to some extent paralleled in the case of Protestant states where nonconformity with the state church has been treated as a political crime. It is, however, noteworthy that from the seventeenth century this reliance of religious groups upon coercion and terror has steadily diminished. The gain of power by the middle classes, the multiplication of Protestant religious groups, the extension of education, the rise of popular government, have combined to disabuse the public mind of its mediæval conviction that heretics are to be exterminated in the interest of the public good. Such policy has now passed over to the antireligious movement of communism. The gospel of proletarian brotherhood is being protected by massacres which surpass those by which the church of the Middle Ages undertook to assure its own existence as a unified group.

IV

It is certainly in no spirit of casuistry that the historian must recognize the fact that idealism, implemented though it may be by brutalities, is still idealism. The persecuting church was none the less the champion of moral values which feudal institutions and absolute monarchies only too readily flouted. The history of the church can never be understood by disregard or over-emphasis of the method of its struggle to perform its function. This history is an illustration of the fact that terror is repeatedly the outcome of sincere efforts for reform. Most of the great terrorists have been idealists possessed of police power. If the mediæval church too easily relied upon the methods of mediæval society in protecting its own integrity, its chief significance did not lie in such methods. It gave new stability to the family, it restrained at least partially the oppression of feudalism, it con-

Christianity and the Morality of Groups

served the influence of classical literature, and has from that day to this, presented a solid front against radical social change. Its history contributes one element of the answer to be given to the problem of group morality. A group devoted to personal values cannot with safety adopt methods opposed to its function. Most of the nations of continental Europe, with their present distrust of democracy and their reliance upon coercion, are the inevitable outcome of a process in which a Christian group has distrusted the power of love which it preached.

It is difficult to find any excuse for persecution on the part of the Christian community. Even if, as is necessary, it be recognized that the constituent members of the church group were under the influence of contemporary brutality, the Christian community cannot escape the charge that it has suffered from the attempt to make the establishment of a church a supreme good. There can be no justification for a Christian group intimidating or coercing others. Historically speaking, religious liberty and religion supported by the state have been shown to be irreconcilable. It is only within

Christianity and Social Process

the last century and a half that the freedom of religious groups from the control of the state has been recognized, and even today newly organized states seek to crush groups that dare to oppose political programs by insisting upon Christian ideals of love.

Such facts are a sad commentary on the inability of humanity to express collectively ideals which are influential in the relations of individuals. It would be unfair to say that inconsistency between the action of a group and the ideals to which its members stand committed is hypocrisy. It may rather be a distorted although sincere conviction that such action is for the benefit of individuals. Plausible support of such conviction is easily found. In most groups there are individuals who wish to exploit the group and must be restrained by force or fear. Such group action is the equivalent of that discipline which every individual must exercise over the elements of his personality which war against his own ideals. Such a restraint, if intelligently exercised, may be an expression of love.

Christianity and the Morality of Groups

V

A more serious question arises in the relation between the various groups themselves. There, as in the case of individuals, there must be a recognition of membership in a larger group composed of at least two groups. If these related groups are to express the Christian ideal of love, each must not only fulfill the function of advancing the welfare of its constituent members, but it must not exploit the individuals of some other group. Humanity must be recognized as greater than its component groups, whether they be classes, nations, or races.

It sounds like the counsel of perfection to say that such relationship should be set up between the innumerable groups in our modern world. That, of course, is the ideal which democracy has set before itself. Democracy, however, becomes increasingly complicated as new groups are organized with highly specialized functions. While, for instance, a New England town was composed very largely of farmers, each living on his own land, democracy as represented by the town meeting was simple. The individual farmers got together in the

Christianity and Social Process

town meeting and adopted by a majority of votes such plans as they desired. When, however, one of these towns grew in population and various industries were introduced, there emerged a series of groups whose interests were not always identical. Furthermore, as America became urbanized and industrialized, the difference of interest among these groups increased greatly. Common action of individuals became increasingly difficult. A study of American politics will illustrate how imperative it is that any attempt at democratic reform recognize the fact that individuals are members of industrial, religious, social, financial, recreational, and a number of other groups. Each one of these groups will exist for the benefit of the individuals who compose it, and often will have interests distinctly opposed to those for which other groups have become organized. Is it possible for the Christian movement to extend its motivation to such groups?

There are those who have given up hope that, however significant the Christian ideals may be for individuals, they are equal to the task of organizing the relationship between groups. The difficulty

Christianity and the Morality of Groups

of such adjustment is certainly not to be denied. But here again clarity of thought demands that we separate the moral attitudes and techniques. When once this has been done we can ask first whether the members of the group and the group itself as a corporate personality are sufficiently moral to act on the basic conviction that the welfare of the individuals must be furthered by the groups. And secondly we can ask whether there is sufficient intelligence to find a way by which the various groups may be so related as to further such welfare. These two questions now confront the social process of the West. While one must recognize the difficulties, loyalty to the basic Christian conception cannot for a moment justify the abandonment of Christian principles and the adoption of a policy of coercion on the part of one group or economic class. Here the basic values embodied in the Christian religion can render supreme help. To doubt the worth of love as a form of coördination of groups is to abandon confidence in the creative processes of the universe itself. Such distrust is certainly not worthy of a brave or intelligent man. He will rather engage in the conscientious search

Christianity and Social Process

for a social technique capable of carrying groups in the direction of larger personal values of individuals. We should sacrifice, not our understanding of the social process, but unintelligent handling of the new differentiations of our social life. This is a rational application of the principle of sacrifice which the Christian church has always made central, but has not always applied to itself or to social evolution. It has been easier to trust to the efficacy of the sacrifices of the Son of God than to make them in the reconstruction of a social order of which the church was a part.

However inconsistent such action on the part of Christians may appear, the recognition of the personal value of individuals does, as in the case of slavery, gradually permeate group action. The most significant effect of cross-fertilization of groups is the organization of a public opinion. This opinion may be stimulated by the action of organized Christian churches, but it is far more due to extension of the educational influence of the Christian group through its members to these other groups. True, their social techniques may be open to criticism. Good people do not always have good

Christianity and the Morality of Groups

sense. But morality extends to techniques. Certain courses of action are seen to be advantageous to the group; certain other courses of action seem to be disadvantageous. Intelligent choice between the two will need motives not grounded in the desire to preserve the *status quo*, but in the extension of personal rights and privileges. Such motives, its history shows, are within the power of the Christian movement to furnish. The sacrifice which the democratizing of any privilege involves can be sustained by religious faith.

The interplay of Christianity with social processes is clearly a social behavior. Until individuals in their varied group relations act in accord with the social implications of their religion, the values within the Christian movement will not be influential in a social process. When such persons, either as individuals or as minorities, take part in group action, Christian values become operative. In some instances such influence will be conservative, protecting by the adoption of wise techniques moral progress already made. In other cases the influence of Christian values will be felt in group actions which tend to produce or direct change.

Christianity and Social Process

The Christian movement has, indeed, been most influential as a social ferment of forces newly released within the cultural process of the West. In the rapid reorganization of the social life of our own day both of these functions of the Christian movement may be exercised. Moral values which have been embodied in group life should be conserved. Readjustments inevitably following from economic and political change should be as far as possible directed away from coercion to peaceful coöperation. Indeed, it may be possible for the Christian movement to develop within existing groups ideals and behavior more in accordance with its own values than minorities within the group may approve. The results of such influence, it is to be hoped, will be felt in a process rather than in a social catastrophe. But such a desirable result will depend upon the readiness of those possessed of privileges to democratize them. In the light of today's rapid changes it seems clear that such democratization must take place. The course proposed by the Christian movement is the course of wisdom. Christianity as a ferment in economic and political change may prevent the miser-

Christianity and the Morality of Groups

ies of group conflict and coerced uniformity. But Christian values will not work automatically; they must be implemented by intelligence in the action of groups. How far this is possible may appear from study of the actual influence of Christianity in the reconstructive periods of Western history.

VI

CHRISTIANITY AND ECONOMICS

THE conviction embodied in the Christian movement that increase in personal value is practicable as a motive for furthering intelligent group morality, is certainly far away from the philosophy of economic determinism. As a form of social behavior Christianity has too often failed to recognize economic evils, but its teachers have uniformly insisted that personal values are superior to the economic. Speaking generally, however, until very recent times the relationship of organized Christianity to the economic elements of the process from which Western civilization has emerged has been negative. It has opposed what it has regarded as economic evils until such opposition has been made futile by the development of new economic situations. In such denunciations the

Christianity and Economics

Christian teachers have been under the sway of the biblical estimate of labor as a curse and of economic theories largely inherited from the non-industrial and non-commercial social order of the Hebrews. The basis for this influence was theological. The Bible was treated as an authority, a revelation from God, and scholastic theology brought to its support the teaching of Aristotle. There was, in consequence, no recognition of the relativity of economic ideals to the structure of the social order. It was not until the seventeenth century that the dominance of these theological ideals was replaced by that of economic theory which, though largely organized by Christians, did not recognize ecclesiastical authority.

I

Christianity as a religious movement was organized in a highly developed civilization, but one in which economic operations were handicapped and debilitated by slavery. It was a civilization practically without machines, and its means of transportation were such elementary ones as sailing and beasts of burden. Commerce, however,

Christianity and Social Process

and to some extent finance, were highly developed and the middle class was growing prosperous as the Empire established peace and trade-routes. Within this social order the Christian church developed with practically no sense of responsibility for improving the economic life. It has, indeed, been alleged that the first Christians were communistic, and certain writers, in the interest of a socialism, have endeavored to make Christianity a proletarian movement. But a sober study of the data does not justify such descriptions. The so-called communism of the early Christian was active emergency relief in which Jews who thought the world was coming to an immediate end endeavored to meet the wants of fellow believers who were out of employment. To speak of such protective charity as communism is quite to misinterpret the situation. The original Christian group did not set up any economic organization. It simply consumed the money that had been contributed for the support of the poor, until the church at Jerusalem itself became the object of charity on the part of the non-Jewish Christian communities founded by Paul. Nor is it true that

Christianity and Economics

the Christians of the second and third centuries were exclusively slaves and poor. Although such persons were in the majority, the church was a fairly representative cross section of society.

The homiletic and theological literature of the early centuries of the Christian movement are full of exhortations to charity as the right use of wealth. The early poverty of the Christians was not permanent. Christians acquired wealth. Persecutions that led to the confiscation of the property of those who refused to deny the Name could not check the growing economic significance of the new movement. The imperial fear of group activity, however, made any application of Christian principles to economic conditions impracticable, if indeed it was thought of. Chrysostom and Ambrose preached something not unlike a common holding of wealth, but there is no evidence that the Christian movement as a whole was affected by such preaching. The one practical protest which radicals in the ancient church made to the evils attendant upon wealth was to retire to some desert or cave. When, later, Benedict organized a monastic order he institutionalized in his demand for poverty the gen-

Christianity and Social Process

eral despair which the Christians had of living a spiritual life in the midst of society. Others were not expected to avoid wealth. They were rather urged to be charitable. Clement of Alexandria, in his interesting little treatise on the salvation of rich men, distinctly objects to poverty as the universal Christian ideal. In a rather clever argument he pleads that if a man were to give away all the property that he had, he would be incapable of obeying the Master's command to give to whoever asked him. In a way this was a compromise with current social practices. Charity as distinct from economic readjustment after the triumph of Constantine became somewhat a national ideal. "It is alien to our character," he declared, "to allow anyone to perish from famine or to be driven to commit so monstrous a crime as the selling of children." But, so far as we know, even after it obtained dominance in the Empire, the Christian church made no attempt to set up any economic program. Its chief aim was the salvation of men after death, the maintenance of individual morality, and the preservation of its own integrity by the organization of correct doctrine. The ideal of eco-

Christianity and Economics

nomic virtue hardly extended beyond the elemental honesty which all commerce demands. The denunciation of oppression on the part of landowners and merchants seems to have had no effect on social life.

II

The attitude of organized Christianity to usury is an interesting illustration of the futility of endeavoring to apply to economic development inhibitions derived from a past social order. Hebraic teaching condemned usury, and on the strength of what was therefore regarded as divine command the Christian teachers for centuries likewise condemned it. The Council of Nicæa decreed that any cleric exacting interest on a loan should be deposed. There is hardly a Church father who failed to denounce the practice. The age of capitalism had not dawned. Mediæval Europe was populated by feudal lords who lived off war or their serfs or military conquest, by peasants, and by men engaged in various trades. Most of the demands for money were, therefore, for purposes of consumption or for agriculture. Loans were permitted to

Christianity and Social Process

meet these demands and by the middle of the thirteenth century the ecclesiastics endeavored to meet the need of such loans through various institutions. At the same time attempts at organizing business were interpreted from the point of view of the poor, and the legislation of the church was affected by the popular hatred of the rich.

The result was that the Jews became the moneylenders of Europe. They were damned in any case, and violation of the teaching of the church did not increase their liabilities in the courts of heaven. To them kings and representatives of cities could go for financial loans or, as frequently happened, for fines and confiscations.

The enormous wealth of the church was not subject to taxation, but was utilized for ecclesiastical undertakings like the building of churches, the support of the clergy, and the maintenance of charities and hospitals. In the course of time this wealth, constantly increased by tithes, took the form of endowments, but these were usually made up of real estate for which rent could be paid. The accumulation of wealth by others than the church was necessary for wars and governmental expendi-

Christianity and Economics

tures of all sorts, but until the development of the cities there was little opportunity for its investment in commercial undertakings. Even in such a case the taking of interest was denounced by canon law and by the authorities of the church. Questions of usury were to be passed on by ecclesiastical courts, although their control continually lessened as secular courts developed. Merchants could accumulate wealth but they were not to lend it. Even thus they were regarded as belonging to the class of those whom Christ drove from the Temple. The desire for wealth was regarded as a form of avarice. When a successful business man died it was to his advantage to leave bequests to the church for masses or ecclesiastical buildings.

III

Later centuries were to show evils which came from the accumulation of wealth by the church, and the possibility of seizing it subsequently became one of the motives of the break of Henry VIII with Rome. The possession of landed property which formerly belonged to the church naturally made the English landowners opposed to

Christianity and Social Process

the reintroduction of the Catholic church, and the consequent restitution of their properties to ecclesiastical institutions. But the attitude of the mediæval church toward wealth and especially toward usury must have been of some protection to the poor. It was one of the causes that prevented the inhabitants of the small towns and villages, especially the agricultural classes, from being crushed by the burden of inherited debt and the tyranny of the money-lender so noticeable among the masses of India. Furthermore, its insistence upon charity and the merits which could be obtained in the courts of heaven by the endowment of religious institutions was an education in altruism which, while by no means absent among the adherents of other religions, was peculiarly adapted to the developing civilization in the West. The Christian movement thus in a way expressed its characteristic values even though sadly hindered by the economic theories of a pre-scientific age.

The attempt of the church to guard society from exploitation by the rich in the matter of usury is to be seen also in the effort to maintain a so-called just price in trade. It was not unlike certain experi-

Christianity and Economics

ments in modern life, but it was not crowned with success, although doubtless it served as a brake on unrestricted competition. The attempt to establish a fixed price regardless of changes in the economic situation of both buyer and seller is obviously exposed to impracticability. Schoolmen were too acute not to recognize this difficulty, and they attempted to find some sort of logical adjustment between abstract ideals and actual situations. The basic position of the church was to the effect that economic life is ideally an expression of neighborly or non-neighborly conduct. Such a view gave partial justification to the struggle of the masses in the later Middle Ages to punish speculators in food. The influence of the church was felt in the various trade guilds, all of which had patron saints who were supposed to grant prosperity on the basis of moral and religious observances.

All these facts show that the church responded to appreciable economic injustices. In so doing, however, it did not undertake to change the basis of European society as organized under feudalism. It did little towards alleviating the condition of the serfs except to insist that they should be treated humanely and as men rather than as tools. It approved of the manumission of serfs and did not in any way attempt to check the economic changes which, especially in England, were developing a genuine yeomanry which was free from feudal exactions. Such an attitude prevented the social classes growing into castes and gave opportunity for the rise of a new economic and political order. In this as in other respects the Christian movement is seen as a more or less appreciable ferment in the evolution of Western civilization.

IV

After the establishment of commercial relations with India and the discovery of America, the economic condition of Europe was radically changed and new social tensions were felt. The increase in the stock of silver served to inflate currencies, with a consequent rise of prices. Commercial primacy began to pass from Italy to states facing the Atlantic. The peasantry, whose situation had been somewhat bettered by the reduction of the number of wage-earners through the ravages of the Black Death, did not share in the new prosperity. On

Christianity and Economics

the contrary, their lot became harder. Discontent was widespread. Opposition to the rich and efforts to free themselves from feudal dues grew into rebellion. Economic groupings emerged without intelligent direction. The lower nobility, especially the German knights, caught between the rising power of the towns and the growth of the holdings of the upper nobility, were also filled with discontent.

The new conditions made banking systems essential to a developing capitalistic system. The denunciation of usury by repeated councils and popes grew anachronistic. Church teachers, however, were equal to the occasion, and with casuistical argument showed that the biblical commands were limited to excessive rather than to normal interest. Thus religious sanction was given to finance and the incipient capitalism was given religious approval.

Little attention and less sympathy were given the needs of the masses. The break of non-Romanized states with the papacy did not involve any radical change in the social structure beyond the establishment of independent states and state

Christianity and Social Process

churches. Instead of a universal church, the Protestants organized churches as aspects of states. They as well as the Roman Church preserved much of the teaching of the past regarding economic matters. Social classes were of God's ordering. The Lutheran movement, springing from feudal and agricultural conditions, was especially conservative. The rising of the peasants, with what seems to modern eyes moderate demands, was as much opposed by Luther as by the princes. The attempt of the Anabaptists to establish a Utopia at Münster was as heartily condemned by him as by the princes who crushed it. The destruction of the Huguenot movement in France had its economic as well as its political and ecclesiastical aspects, and the consequent rise of the English woolen industry laid the foundation for the development of the political influence of Protestantism.

It is impossible to discover any large influence of the Christian movement in these various changes. It certainly did not try to reorganize social relations. While it is true that ecclesiastical enmities were active in struggles for political and economic mastery, no serious appeal was made to

Christianity and Economics

the ideals of Jesus for initiating social adjustment. Ecclesiastical minorities and individual teachers, however, felt concern over the new economic conditions and, within the limits of prevalent economic theory, tried to find some means of relieving the masses. It would not be altogether accurate to describe such policy as one of conscious compromise, although compromise was present. Actual situations had to be faced, and the churches as forms of organized social behavior within a social process were not ready to incite revolution.

v

Perhaps as good an illustration as any of the relation of the Christian movement to the economic development of Western civilization is the relation of Calvinism to capitalism. The most superficial study of history discloses the striking fact that the modern capitalistic organization of society had its origin among people who, like the Huguenots, the Dutch, the English, and the Americans, have been Calvinists. There has been no little discussion as to whether capitalism is due to their Calvinistic outlook upon life. While no final

Christianity and Social Process

answer to such a question can be given, it is certainly true that both capitalism and Calvinism are akin in that each seeks to find a solid basis for security. The sixteenth and seventeenth centuries were struggles of the champions of the *status quo* in politics and religion with those who represented new economic and political trends. The need for some secure basis of protection of oneself was consequently everywhere apparent. In a period when commerce was developing, the accumulation of wealth for the furtherance of business was indispensable for economic security. In the political world at the same time the one basis for a social order was that of the irresponsible absolute monarchy. The area and the peoples in which these two tendencies were most pronounced naturally came under the influence of each. Calvinism as a religious system developed self-control, honesty, prudence, and thrift, virtues particularly applicable to a period of economic change. It also brought into the entire range of life a conviction that God's will was supreme and, therefore, that obedience to his law would make social life secure. Unlike Lutheranism, Calvinism sprang from urban conditions and did not oppose commerce or finance. Work was ordained by God and, though the punishment of sin, was to be made a source of wealth which could be used in God's service. Men were to get, keep and give wealth. While acquisitiveness lay within such psychology, a sense of security did result.

Unless I mistake the signs of the times, a similar tension is to be seen in our day. We have lost our confidence that wealth can produce security even for itself, and the absolute sovereignty of the seventeenth-century theologian is all but deposed by democratic and scientific changes. The consequent feeling of insecurity is vastly more than a question of orthodoxy; it is a general uncertainty as to whether love and coöperation are a practical basis upon which to build economic life. Beside this every other issue seems incidental. Can men be trusted to coöperate sincerely for their own well-doing, or must groups be coerced into doing that which is to their advantage? Will modern men and women be able to see in the universe a supreme moral will comparable with the sovereign

Christianity and Social Process

God of Calvinism? It is the great task of the church to enable them to see it.

VI

One major element of progress to which the Christian movement must now adapt itself is the emergence of economic groups because of the use of natural forces to replace human labor. Christianity in its older form had no such difficulty. Machines had not been invented and capitalism included land and slaves. So long as such a social order continued, Christian morality was comparatively simple. Rights of property had to be regarded, and labor was considered as, on the whole, imperative. When, later, the commercial class arose thrift became a dominant motive and the tendency toward mass capital was appreciable. But with the beginning of the industrial revolution in approximately the middle of the eighteenth century, an entirely new grouping emerged. The serf and the slave were replaced by the wage-earner. The dominant notion of property, however, was not changed; labor was treated as a commodity rather than as a personal contribution to the pro-

Christianity and Economics

ductive process, and the employer was a master. One has only to read the religious literature of the latter part of the eighteenth century and the early part of the nineteenth, to see that the morality which the church enforced was conditioned by unquestioned acceptance of economic inheritances.

In the early days of the Industrial Revolution there was a distinct effort to prevent by violence the introduction of machinery. Such a reaction was natural, but served hardly more than to consolidate the enmity between the owners of the machines and those who tended them. There seems to have been no serious understanding of the numerous social changes that followed the appearance of machinery. The evil influences of class stratification were apparent in the early years of England's industrial development, and formed a mold within which for many years the idealism implicit in the Christian movement was shaped. The church as an institution seems to have taken little interest in the growing discontent of the working-class until the rise of a little group of men known as the Christian Socialists, chief among whom were Frederick Dennison Maurice and Charles Kingsley. Under

Christianity and Social Process

their inspiration and leadership a clearer perception of the situation developed, and distinct efforts were made to give the laborer new opportunity for education. The new social conscience led to legislation giving more rights to the laboring party, but the church as an institution took little interest in such matters. It centred its efforts upon the development of philanthropy and conventional morality which did not attempt to change the existing structure of the society. What was true of England was true of other sections of the Western World.

Although the Christian movement in the first stages of the industrial transformation was engaged in preserving the moral ideals which were unaffected by changes in the economic life, in the latter part of the nineteenth century groups of churchmen became interested in the scientific study of society, and immediately began agitation for the extension of the moral concepts of the teaching of Jesus to economic conditions. Thus there grew up what was commonly known as the social gospel, which has been bitterly opposed by ultraconservative groups within the Christian church.

Christianity and Economics

VII

Recently the social significance of the introduction of machinery has attracted serious attention. Now, as never before, is it clear that the problem is something more than mere economic efficiency. Where machines replace men, what is to be done with the men? The problem of unemployment becomes an element of the total social problem. How will these men and women, whose labor the machine has made no longer necessary, live? Can there be employment found for them or made for them? Must they be supported by the dole? Must the community set up public works? Should the number of hours of persons who labor be decreased so that more men can be employed? Can two people, working half time and so producing what one man could produce in full time, live on the amount of a single man's wages? If they cannot, must the standard of living be lowered or must wages and consequent prices be raised? How shall nations where the standard of living is low, but technical efficiency is high, be prevented from ruinous competition? Clearly, all such questions

Christianity and Social Process

cannot be answered wisely by those who are indifferent to the human elements involved. There is a basic need that human rather than economic welfare should be final. Just how this moral attitude should best express itself is a matter of intelligence. But society has not really become moral until personal considerations are superior to the strictly economic. And at this point the influence of the church should be distinct and effective. If it be necessary to slow down the expansion of the machine age in the interests of a more gradual and so a more healthful adjustment of new economic conditions, it should be the attitude of the church to stimulate the moral sensibility of its members and others whom it may influence to adopt a line of development which denies the right of individual producers to disintegrate the social order in the interest of industrial efficiency.

But the moral aspects of the replacement of manual labor by machines have been by no means limited to the matter of employment. There is the enormously important question of the effect of leisure upon those who, by virtue of mechanical efficiency, are not obliged to work so many hours

Christianity and Economics

as formerly. The probability is that men's characters are mostly set by their behavior when they are not under compulsion to perform definite tasks. A social order where the wage-earner would work thirty hours a week rather than sixty or seventy at once raises the question as to what shall be done during the leisure hours. Here again are a question of morality and a question of techniques. Men need to see the importance of these periods which give opportunity for self-directive conduct. If they become simply opportunities for loafing or for a search for amusement, the leisure will very likely become an occasion of personal deterioration. If, however, society comes to feel the moral responsibility for the right use of leisure time, a civilization may be greatly developed and the welfare of the individual be made more certain.

Ignorance and indifference on the part of organized Christians have been greatly modified during the last generation. In the latter days of the nineteenth century the study of the life and teaching of Jesus resulted in a new conception of the applicability of his teaching to social as well as individual morality. Doubtless interest of leaders in

Christianity and Social Process

this organization of the social gospel was stimulated by Socialism, but not many of them were Socialists. Most of the writing was done by professors in theological seminaries, and the new significance of Christianity was very greatly extended. In the United States the various religious bodies appointed Social Service Commissions which issued literature and undertook to maintain something like organized religious instruction in social affairs within the churches. The Social Creed of the churches was drawn up by the Federal Council of Churches of Christ in America, and this in its various later forms has been adopted by many of the religious denominations. In England the development of this interest in social affairs on the part of the churches became very active, and is to be seen in many organizations: probably the most significant is the Conference on Politics, Economics, and Citizenship, commonly known as Copec. In Stockholm, in 1925 was held the Universal Conference on Christian Life and Work which distinctly faced the issues set by industry. Its pronouncements were anything but radical, but it at least showed that there was developing among the various Christian groups a unity of interest in the moral aspects of the economic life. Indeed, the social interests of Christians are at the present time highly developed and the number of organizations devoted to propounding the social significance of Jesus is almost countless.

VIII

The question may naturally be raised why the condition of the world is what it is. Two replies are possible. In the first place, there is sin, both individual and social. Vast numbers of men and women are selfish, unwilling to make the sacrifices which the humanizing of the economic processes demands. Even when groups representing the same economic interests undertake to draw up codes for their own conduct, they have had difficulty in enforcing their ideals. The principles of Jesus no more than the principles of any other teacher have magical power. They will not work unless people are ready to make them dominant elements of their behavior.

The second answer is that social sciences have not yet developed techniques which can unquali-

Christianity and Social Process

fiedly be adopted by Christian groups. Progress, however, has been made in these regards, and the general principle has been repeatedly illustrated that a technique becomes a moral issue when it is clearly seen to be the best available. A comparison of the recent pronouncements of the various Christian bodies with those made a generation ago will disclose the advance that has been made in implementing values. The churches by resolutions have set themselves squarely in support of shortened working-days, group bargaining, adult labor. Opposition on the part of interested groups continues, but the very pressure of circumstances is showing that a larger recognition of human values in industry is imperative if civilization is not to fall into a welter of revolutions.

The issue is too complicated to be left in the hands of any single body within the state. The development of economic groups like trade unions and employers' associations, despite their initial controversies, undoubtedly makes toward the maintenance of human values, and the Christian communities in an increasingly more intelligent way are giving motives to the proper adjustment

Christianity and Economics

of group interests. Even when this influence is denied, the ideals which economic groups profess are those for which Christians have stood. Where the economic life is free from this atmospheric pressure of an intelligent Christian idealism, human relations are still suffering. The world at large is not ready to commit itself to major premises of economic theory which are not based on human experience, and the building up of morals in the economic world is to a very considerable extent opportunist. But it is none the less in process. Whether the constructive forces will find capitalist groups sufficiently intelligent to be ready to democratize privilege and treat wage-earners as partners in the productive process remains to be seen. Humanity does not seem to be naturally generous, and the transformation of human nature from acquisitiveness to economic coöperation is difficult. The neglect of the principle of sacrifice, which Jesus so clearly saw was involved in that personal coöperation which he called love, continues to prevent the betterment of our economic relations. It is the business of every religion to convince the world of sin, of righteousness, and

Christianity and Social Process

of judgment. The building up of more intelligent morals is certainly regarded as a primary interest in the Christian movement. The Christian principle of love applied to economic groups stands over against revolutionary coercion. The Christian religion emphasizes a moral process which does not stand committed to an economic philosophy. So far as one can see from the rather obscure teachings of history, the moralizing of existing institutions rather than revolution is the preferable and less destructive course, but in one way or another efforts will be made to establish human values above economic efficiency. It is a terrible indictment of any religion if it shows itself incapable of such intelligent extension of its moral ideals, and if, like the orthodox church of Russia, it must be destroyed in order that human values may be forwarded.

Similarly, in other aspects of our economic life the issue is one of morality rather than of efficiency. The world might very well stop the development of industrial efficiency and declare a moratorium on improvements in machinery for a generation. Perhaps in that period it might learn

Christianity and Economics

how to adjust the personal and impersonal values of society. But such proposals are in the nature of the case rhetorical. We cannot stop the development of the machine and the complications of our financial world. One thing that Christians must undertake is to reorganize them so that human values will be preserved. We came to the edge of the abyss in 1933, and we are not yet sure that we have found a practical road to real recovery. But one thing seems to be universally admitted—that no complete recovery and readjustment of human values in the machine age will be possible until the economic development is dominated by a spirit of coöperation which has been altogether lacking in the past. How great is the change in this regard can be seen by the recent economic developments within the United States, where the policy of a generation ago to prevent the development of trusts has been replaced by the segregation of dominant elements of the industrial world under the direction of the federal government itself. But the success of such a reorganization depends largely upon the readiness of the various groups involved to sacrifice profits in the interest of the general good. The fact that such good-will is not fully exhibited explains the need of legal coercion. But the emphasis upon coöperation is another testimony to the validity of the principle of love which Christianity, despite the blunderings and selfishness of Christians, has embodied and which it is its mission to evoke.

VII

CHRISTIANITY
AND INTERNATIONALISM

THE general relation of the Christian movement to other elements of the social order of the West will serve as an approach to the consideration of its relationship with political groups. The history of such relationship is not difficult to trace. For three centuries Christianity was an unlicensed religion within the Roman Empire. The refusal of Christians to sacrifice to the emperor was naturally regarded as political disloyalty, and Christian communities were subjected to intermittent and generally local persecutions which in the latter part of the third century culminated in an attempt on the part of Decius and Domitian to extirpate the religion. But Christians had become too numerous and too influential because of char-

Christianity and Social Process

acter and wealth and organization for such an attempt to succeed. Constantine, recognizing the political value of the church, became its supporter. From his day, with the exception of the brief reign of Julian, the relations of the church to the Empire were intimate. Councils were able to utilize the power of the state to enforce their decisions against heretics. Parties to theological controversies were favored or opposed by the emperors. On the other hand, the power of the church as the channel of supernatural grace was repeatedly exercised to check the cruelty of the emperors. The power of the bishop of Rome increased greatly as the empire weakened.

After the collapse of the Western Empire, Christianity was adopted by the various tribes who settled in western Europe. The theology of some of these tribes was at the start Arian rather than orthodox, but with the triumph of the Franks, the church of Rome became inextricably joined with the political development of Europe. Bishops and abbots became feudal lords. The question whether they should be appointed by the emperors and kings or by the pope was settled in the long War

Christianity and Internationalism

of Investitures by a concordat which gave religious and political authorities joint power of appointment of ecclesiastics to their fiefs. Innumerable bitter struggles arose from this arrangement, but, again speaking generally, its success in retaining administration of its growing property and feudal rights, made the church its own master and so conserved values which had spiritual vitality. On the other hand, the development of the political power of the church, as has already been pointed out, led to its utilizing the state for the preservation of its theological and group solidarity. Until the rise of Protestantism it should be remembered that the church was exclusively the clergy, and in it, as in the contemporary political units, policies and programs were largely determined by individuals or groups of those possessing ecclesiastical authority. With the rise of nations churches became phases of the states, and in consequence ecclesiastical differences figured in international disputes.

Until most recent times, throughout the entire history of Western civilization churches have not undertaken to develop any systematic morality for international relations. On the contrary, they have

Christianity and Social Process

been agents of international enmities. True, various popes undertook to prevent wars, but the priest and the pastor became the champions of the state. The church prayed for peace, but its official prayer did not include the national recognition of the rights of other nations. As a form of social behavior it found its technique in current practices and attitudes. Only in the case of small sects was there any attempt to express the teaching of Jesus in political life, and in the case of these sects nonparticipation in civic affairs usually seemed the only way in which that teaching could be expressed. International relations were thus left to the decision of those who bore the sword.

I

For the first time in history international relations are forcing us to consider the possibility of national morality. Such an interest was inevitable in view of the intimacies developed by our new means of communication, transportation, and the establishment of world markets. The modern nation is now intensely self-conscious. Indeed, it is probable that the discussion of international debts

Christianity and Internationalism

has contributed largely to a way of thinking about a nation as if it were an individual debtor or creditor. That anthropomorphism which so determines our thought of what is neither individual nor personal is particularly influential in the discussion of international finance. However the accountant may deal with national incomes and outgoes, the foreigner looks at the creditor or debtor nation in much the same way as he looks at debtors and creditors in his own economic relations. We have Uncle Sam and John Bull.

But is such anthropomorphism really safe? Can a nation be brought within the categories of morality? The history of Western civilization does not warrant any very confident answer to such a question. It has not been difficult to personify the nation in a monarch, and notwithstanding the aphorism that kings can do no wrong, moral judgments have been passed over the action of national rulers. And of recent years the possibility of thus identifying a nation with a single ruler has not grown less. Nationalism in its most recent form has dramatized patriotism in dominant personalities who have replaced the parliaments.

Christianity and Social Process

There is no evidence, however, that the growth of either a poetic or a realistic national individualism has made the question of national morality easier to answer. Except for the sentimentalist, rhetoric is not a safe basis for generalization. Yet the poetic practice of seeing the relations of nations as those of individuals is altogether too common to be neglected. Our emotions make no small contribution to social action. The development of a national attitude is not difficult, provided that such an attitude can capitalize a discontent, and by clever propaganda transform discontent into hatred. If people hate together, they will act together. The psychology of war makes this sinister observation only too plausible. But just as there can be no unity among those persons in whom mutual hatreds are dominant, so in international affairs to develop national unity by arousing international hatred is a threat of disturbance, with war as the outcome.

Many Christian writers assert that the principles of the Sermon on the Mount should be and can be applied to nations. With this I am in profound agreement, but at the same time I recognize the difficulties which the hope involves. For beneath it

Christianity and Internationalism

lies the basic question as to whether a nation can be treated as a moral entity in the same sense that the individual can be so treated.

Upon the answer to that question must depend any constructive program in the building up of international peace. If national organization is incompatible with morality, it is idle to attempt to develop international good-will and international peace. But that would mean that the whole process of integration and coördination which marks the cosmic process and has expressed itself in the case of human individuals has ceased to operate.

Such a conclusion is impossible for one who has confidence in the cosmic process itself. Here, as in all other relations of human beings, the congruity of love with that which is cosmically ultimate makes international morality less a dream of the sentimentalist than a goal for human endeavor. To enforce this conviction is one aspect of Christianity as a form of social behavior.

II

At this point we enter a field of endeavor where precedents are almost lacking. The relations of nations with each other have always been those

Christianity and Social Process

of hostility modified by treaties. Only in the case of individual thinkers like Grotius has religion been regarded as more than an aid to the state. So long as there is no community of action there can be no morality. Where there is the presupposition that a final arbitrament will be that of force, religion can be of little influence except to sanctify enmities. Individual relations have passed through this stage in mediæval Europe, where decisions were reached by duels conducted under the sanction of the church. In the relations of individuals judicial process has replaced these trials by combat, but in the relations of nations such intelligent procedure is yet in the making. Until there can be developed a public opinion which distrusts war or the fear of war as the only basis of international agreement, and international politics sufficiently recognizes the interpenetration of national interests in a world every day growing more interdependent economically, national morality is impossible. So long as religion is a phase of national policy and a religious organization is the agent of government, efforts at international good-will get little help from official religious action.

Christianity and Internationalism

We find ourselves confused by the persistence of the older ideals of government as distinct from the governed. The state has too often been an end in itself, and its real function as that of a social group, organized for the purpose of furthering the welfare of its constituent elements, has been neglected. Indeed, national morality is the most complicated form of group morality. And it must be admitted that any moral individuality of a nation differs from that of the individual in this particular regard. The state, like any social group, should be not an end but an instrument. It exists for the protection of its members. In the performance of that duty it has always felt justified in taking actions which in the case of individuals would be regarded as immoral. Furthermore, it is becoming customary, in theory at least, to hold that the church is to keep its hands off politics just as the state must keep its hands off religion. In consequence, religious leaders have feared to set forth the moral aspects of citizenship with sufficient earnestness and intelligence. While it is admitted that there should be a separation between the church and the state, there should not be a

Christianity and Social Process

separation between the citizen and the state. Religion ought to create a moral reserve upon which politics can draw. The moral education of the individual must include his obligation to the common life of the nation. But such obligation is decidedly more than a passive response to political policies. The values set forth in the Christian movement must carry over into the political group. If the attitude of good-will can be presumed as conditioning the action of the state, the problem of how it can find expression becomes a matter of political intelligence.

At this point, however, it is necessary to bear in mind that the morality of a group cannot be established by atomistic nations. In any group morality there must be a group of groups. But the *mores* of such a super-group will be relative to the purposes of its constituent groups. That is to say, there is mutual obligation. The action of one nation cannot be wholly independent of the action of another nation. Nationalism, if once made moral, would be an immense aid in the development of a happier world. If there is to be any international morality there must be a group life of

Christianity and Internationalism

nations within which national *mores* can be organized. In the case of nations as in that of individuals morality will be a social product. This fact, however, will not be clearly seen until public opinion in the various nations has itself become morally educated. Citizens must feel that the functions of their nation to care for their welfare are not safely separable from similar functions on the part of other nations. Such an attitude of mind would be obviously at one with the basic conception of Christianity.

III

Christianity, no more than any other religion, is something apart from human beings. Only as men and women make the ideals of the Christian movement operative in their own behavior will such ideals actually affect social process. Much discussion about the relation of international affairs ignores this very simple but important fact. One would think from much of this discussion that Christianity was a force existing outside of humanity instead of a religious movement composed of the same persons who are in other social

Christianity and Social Process

relations. It is human beings who distrust the applicability of love to international affairs.

National groups are so large that it is hard to find the proper balance between the duties of a group to its members and its relations with similar groups who in turn must provide for their own members. How bewildering is this task appears in the various international conferences and the tensions within the League of Nations. Despite the treaties that reject war as a basis of international policy, there are vast numbers of citizens of every country who distrust the citizens of other countries. Any call for the abatement of national ambitions is interpreted as insincere. Nations benefited by other nations very easily come to regard such assistance as their right. Such distrust is unfortunately difficult to eradicate. The precedents of history are against the possibility of any international relationship which is genuinely moral. Even those who believe that international morality is practicable find it difficult to believe that a national government would be fulfilling its function as protector of the welfare of its subjects if it completely disarmed while other nations were

Christianity and Internationalism

armed. Into this highly disputed matter I do not propose to go, except to say that I cannot see that the death of Christ on the cross has any parallel with the destruction of a nation. True, a moral nation would be ready to be sacrificial, but the principle of love, when applied to national affairs, will be that of the coördination of privilege within an international group rather than some form of national asceticism. National non-resistance and surrender may at times be wiser than conflict, but it by no means follows that such a policy assures the full realization of the ideals of Jesus. A conquered nation may be as full of hatred without fighting as with fighting.

The thoughtful Christian cannot, however, abandon the conviction that the application of the principle of love to international affairs as in the relation of all groups, would result in a vast increase in human welfare. Such a faith is something more than a belief in an absence of fighting. A warless world might be anything but a happy world. International peace which is a mere preservation of the *status quo* set by war is certainly not an adequate expression of the principle of intelligent group action. Far more important than peace is the establishment of relations which lead to international good will. Here we meet questions which seem at the start far removed from international conflict. But if we are to have a warless world we must change those situations from which wars arise. Interracial hatreds, the inheritance of past injustice, the establishment of tariffs and quotas, the struggle for the control of territory possessed of oil or coal or other valuable deposits, the dumping of surplus products on the markets of other nations, journalism that arouses national jealousies, all these are elements of international situations that must be adjusted in some intelligent way if there is to be anything like national morality. Economic retaliation is as hostile to the basic principles of Christianity as is any other form of attempt to do injury. We are not yet sufficiently intelligent or international-minded to discover ways by which governments can promote the welfare of their own citizens without decreasing the welfare of the citizens of other nations. The technique for such adjustment lags behind even

Christianity and Internationalism

the idealism of those who believe in the practicability of international good will.

As an illustration of how Christian idealism fails to modify political policy, reference can be made to the pronouncement of the Holy Alliance which has all the fervor of religious faith:

> "In the name of the Most Holy and Indivisible Trinity: Holy Alliance of Sovereigns of Austria, Prussia, and Russia. Their Majesties the Emperor of Austria, the King of Prussia, and the Emperor of Russia, having, in consequence of the great events which have marked the course of the three last years in Europe, and especially of the blessings which it has pleased Divine Providence to shower down upon those States which place their confidence and their hope on it alone, acquired the intimate conviction of the necessity of settling the steps to be observed by the Powers, in their reciprocal relations, upon the sublime truths which the Holy Religion of our Saviour teaches; They solemnly declare that the present Act has no other object than to publish, in the face of the whole world, their fixed resolution, both in the administration of their respective States, and in

their political relations with every other Government, to take for their sole guide the precepts of that Holy Religion, namely, the precepts of Justice, Christian Character, and Peace, which, far from being applicable only to private concerns, must have an immediate influence on the councils of Princes, and guide all their steps, as being the only means of consolidating human institutions and remedying their imperfections. In consequence, their Majesties have agreed on the following Articles:—

Art. I. Conformably to the words of the Holy Scriptures, which command all men to consider each other as brethren, the Three contracting Monarchs will remain united by the bonds of a true and indissoluble fraternity, and considering each other as fellow countrymen, they will, on all occasions and in all places, lend each other aid and assistance; and, regarding themselves towards their subjects and armies as fathers of families, they will lead them, in the same spirit of fraternity with which they are animated, to protect Religion, Peace, and Justice.

Art. II. In consequence, the sole principle of force, whether between the said Govern-

Christianity and Internationalism

ments or between their Subjects, shall be that of doing each other reciprocal service, and of testifying by unalterable good will the mutual affection with which they ought to be animated, to consider themselves all as members of one and the same Christian nation; the three allied Princes looking on themselves as merely delegated by Providence to govern three branches of the one family, namely, Austria, Prussia, and Russia, thus confessing that the Christian world, of which they and their people form a part, has in reality no other Sovereign than Him to whom alone power really belongs, because in Him alone are found all the treasures of love, science, and infinite wisdom, that is to say, God, our Divine Saviour, the Word of the Most High, the Word of Life. Their Majesties consequently recommend to their people, with the most tender solicitude, as the sole means of enjoying that Peace which arises from a good conscience, and which alone is durable, to strengthen themselves every day more and more in the principles and exercise of the duties which the Divine Saviour has taught to mankind.

Art. III. All the Powers who shall choose

solemnly to avow the sacred principles which have dictated the present Act, and shall acknowledge how important it is for the happiness of nations, too long agitated, that these truths should henceforth exercise over the destinies of mankind all the influence which belongs to them, will be received with equal ardour and affection into this Holy Alliance. Done in triplicate, and signed at Paris, the year of Grace 1815, 14-26th, September."

The actual significance of this Alliance was an attempt to prevent the spread of democracy, which led to the Monroe Doctrine of the United States.

IV

Before international morality can be organized a society of nations is indispensable. Such a society should be more than a League of Nations or some sort of super-state with its courts and police. I mean a social group of nations accustomed to act in such a way as individuals act in their groups. Such a society cannot be immediately formed. If it ever comes into existence it will be the result of a long process in which nations acquire habits of

Christianity and Internationalism

living together. The good will within such nations will always be threatened by individuals who, because of unintelligent nationalism, will endeavor to isolate a nation from its fellows. Whether the Christian churches or the various organizations of Christians outside the churches can arouse a co-operative national opinion in Western civilization remains to be seen. But nationalism cannot be made moral in any other way than by the recognition of the moral aspects of citizenship. Certain advances have been made along the line of such ideals in various conferences and treaties, but we are still confronted with the difficulties of economic adjustment. For the present one has to say regretfully that we are neither sufficiently internationally-minded nor intelligent to adopt methods which enable the individuals of one nation to share in the privileges of another. Morality will be a torso until international *mores* are developed.

There is no short cut to such morality. National unities are not going to be destroyed that all individuals shall be subjects of a universal state. But if human history has any lesson for us, it is that humanity advances in groups rather than as

Christianity and Social Process

individuals, and that groups get their significance as they further the welfare and freedom of their constituent members. Nationalism may under proper influences become coöperative. International morality would then be a morality between nations.

If one comes to the consideration of the development of the moral quality of the nation from a study of other types of morality, the situation is not so hopeless as would appear from a conventional discussion. A morality is the outgrowth of group action and commonly accepted practices. Time is an essential element of the process involved, and in this regard one cannot look back over the years which have passed since the war without having the disappointments which hope has suffered somewhat tempered by the sucsession of attempts at group action. And this notwithstanding the fact that the results of the various conferences have not overcome the inertia of century-old practices and attitudes. For the first time in history men have actually undertaken to bring international relations into the field of discussion rather than of threatened war. The abject con-

Christianity and Internationalism

dition of the world has aided in such an attempt to avoid appeal to force. The magnitude of humanity's tragedy has taught a lesson which incidental wars and amoral internationalism could not teach. Men undertook to live as if the welfare of individuals were less important than a national policy and the protection of material wealth. The coördinating process of the universe which makes toward ever more complicated and personal group life was ignored and flouted. The resulting economic worldwide depression is also a depression of spirit. It cannot be remedied except as men live in accordance with the cosmic process itself. This obligation extends not only to the individuals, but to economic classes and nations. There is no avoiding this cosmic process. There is no way to coöperate with it except in peaceful furthering of personal welfare. Human life has reached the point where either great combinations such as nations must work together in mutual trust or precipitate misery.

Such a conclusion is reached by all observers. The only question which seems to be left to be answered is whether humanity will make the sort

Christianity and Social Process

of choice that makes toward destruction or toward human welfare. It is the business of Christians, as of all those in other religions who have similar confidence in love, to see that the decision shall be made for human welfare, and that individuals, classes, and nations make such adjustments and sacrifices as will assure success to intelligent techniques of international coöperation.

v

Closely associated with the problem of international relations is revolution. The part which the Christian church has had in periods of revolutionary psychology has been usually conservative. In Roman Catholic countries the weight of religion has been thrown on the maintenance of the *status quo* and the church as in France and Russia has suffered. In Protestant countries there has been no violent revolution unless we so consider the recent movements in Germany and the rebellion of the American Colonies against England. At the time of the French Revolution there were decided discontent and threatened popular movements in England, but the rise of the Methodist

Christianity and Internationalism

movement diverted attention from politics to religion and tempered the discontent of the working classes. John Wesley can hardly be called a democrat in the political sense, but the influence of the movement which he inaugurated was undoubtedly in the direction of democracy. The evangelical movement in the Church of England also can be seen to have been one of the causes why the furor which the early stages of the French Revolution developed subsided without organizing violent opposition to the existing form of government.

The revolutionary movements in Europe and Asia of late have sprung largely from communists who are opposed to religion as an anesthetic of capitalism. In the case of Russia, the opposition of the church to constitutional reform was too flagrant to permit the revolutionists and the church people to deny it.

On the continent of Europe there has been close affiliation between the Roman Catholic Church and politics; the Center Party in Germany, for instance, was entirely Catholic. Both Germany and France have attempted to prevent the entrance of the church into political affairs, but unsuccess-

Christianity and Social Process

fully. In Italy the pope has recovered some of his old territorial political rights, and the church has been made responsible for certain aspects of the life of the nation. The present revolutionary movement in Spain is too recent for one to form any definite opinion as to whether the Socialist Republic will be forced to retrace some of its anti-ecclesiastical actions. In the case of the Protestant states the liberty of religion has been gradually won, although it is now threatened in Germany. It would probably be accurate to say that in the earlier struggles which, with the exception of the civil wars in England, hardly reached the level of a revolution, the state churches were champions of the *status quo* and the nonconformist churches represented the rising tide of democracy. Within recent years, however, leaders within the state churches have stood boldly for the extension of political and economic privileges.

Only in rare instances have there been revolutionary attempts to make religion a basis for a Protestant state. Perhaps the most striking illustrations of this would be the short-lived Anabaptist state at Münster and the Congregational theocracy

Christianity and Internationalism

of the early Colonial days in New England. In the latter case the effort to make suffrage depend upon church membership proved a failure.

VI

The influence of the Christian movement upon war has varied. The religious motive was largely present in the Crusades, and these were marked by brutality which was not limited to the treatment of Saracens, but resulted in the sacking of Constantinople and the massacre of the Albigenses. Wiclif, despite his noble efforts for a more Christlike Christianity, approved wars waged in the cause of the church or for the honor of Christ. After the rise of the national states in Europe, their political ambitions found ecclesiastical enmities their ally, and for generations the Catholics and Protestants fought with a bitterness which all but depopulated Germany. Yet on the other hand it is true that the papacy frequently intervened in private and public wars. Benedict XII was pursuing a recognized policy of the popes when he endeavored to bring peace to feudal states in order that a united Europe might fight the

Christianity and Social Process

Turks. Both Benedict and other popes opposed arbitration by secular authorities, claiming the supreme right to mediate between quarreling kings. Boniface VIII succeeded in temporarily preventing war between France and England. Yet no pope appears to have been a theoretical pacifist. It was wrong for Christians to fight each other, but war against heretics and unbelievers was commendable. A Crusade would serve to stop the private wars of Christian princes. And after his Crusade was abandoned, Benedict was partially successful in his efforts to promote peace between various kings.

The "truce of God" declared that from the evening of Wednesday to the morning of Monday there should be no fighting; also from the beginning of Advent to the first Sunday after Epiphany. During the later Middle Ages the churches undertook to mitigate the practices of war, especially as regards the killing of women and children and the pillaging of towns. But it is a matter of regret that these merciful limitations found little observance in the terrible wars of the sixteenth and seventeenth centuries. Yet even

Christianity and Internationalism

during that brutal period there were many Christian people who opposed war. Interesting enough, the first organization of the moral law governing the relation of nations in a world no longer one under the pope came from the Spanish Catholic jurist, Franciscus di Vittoria. Later the Spanish jurist Suarez declared that each state, "viewed in relation to the human race, is in some measure a member of that universal unity." Sir Thomas More, in his *Utopia*, conceives of a warless republic. Most important is the celebrated Hugo Grotius of Holland, father of international law. His motive was not only juridical, but profoundly religious. Probably at no time before the present has there ever been a more aggressive nationalism than in the seventeenth century. Grotius relied not only upon the law of nature, but on religious considerations. He concludes his great work on the *Law of War and Peace* with the fervent prayer, "May God write these lessons—here none can—on the hearts of all those who have the affairs of Christendom in their hands; and may he give to those persons a mind fit to understand and to respect rights, human and divine, and lead them to

Christianity and Social Process

recollect always that the ministration committed to them is no less than this, that they are governors of man, a creature most dear to God."

But Grotius' influence, unfortunately, was not great enough to offset that combination of nationalism and religion which swept so murderously across Europe in the seventeenth century. Yet even then, the Society of Friends had begun its long-lived protest against war in the name of the Gospel. Various Christian writers also, under the influence of Grotius, undertook to apply the ideals of the Gospel to national affairs, but failed to mitigate that belligerent nationalism that made war a means for the development of rival states.

VII

That it is the business of the Christian religion to prevent a collapse of civilization is expressly denied by many Christians. To them civilization is beyond regeneration and the only basis of hope is the return of Christ from heaven and his establishment by miraculous power, the triumph of righteousness, the binding of Satan, and the eternal separation of the evil and the good. That such an

Christianity and Internationalism

outlook upon life was possessed by the people of the New Testament period seems undeniable, but the history of the Christian movement has never been set by such beliefs. However slow the Christian forces may have been in furthering reform, reforms have always been consolidated and inspired by the ferment of the Christian ideals. Something like this can be seen to be already in process. Whether or not the Christian church can be credited for initiating the opposition to war, it is beyond question that at the present time Christians are among the most outspoken champions of international peace. Practically all the peace societies and foundations are representative of religious interests. The proposed World Conference on International Peace Through Religion is planned as the outcome of a movement which already has its representatives in many countries, including India and Japan. Whether or not this moral and religious support is at present equal to creating a public opinion that will affect diplomats and conferences remains to be seen, but it seems beyond doubt that unless the representatives of economic and nationalist tendencies realize that

Christianity and Social Process

isolation is less efficient than coöperation, the only hope for avoiding a new, unparalleled tragedy will be that the poverty of the nations will be so complete as to make war financially impossible. The development of nationalism is universal, but its moral significance varies greatly. It has, however, always one marked characteristic: a nation should be economically self-sufficient. To this end tariffs are established and the various devices of international banking and propaganda are used to consolidate the distrust, if not the hatred, of other nations. Certainly such atomistic patriotism is not in accord with the basic ideals of the Christian morality. Just as certain is it that the religious organizations of the different countries are incapable of preventing the rise of this new national feeling. Christians should undertake to prevent nationalism from taking the place of religion. They must make it moral and coöperative rather than atomistic and acquisitive. They can help to develop an internationalism which will not be that of an economic class, but of nations themselves. A recognition of the significance of group morality will bring political units into some sort of co-

Christianity and Internationalism

operative relation in which each nation will become a participant in an international relationship which will further the well-being of its constituent nations. Such a condition of affairs seems almost beyond the range of a realistic view of modern life, and yet, as one sets the present in the long perspective of history, it is possible to see that the development of political self-consciousness is now partially subject to controls and idealistic influences which the past lacked. When one considers the various influences which are operating to bring about such changes, it is evident that the Christian religion now, as in the past, has the opportunity of giving certain moral direction and backing to the creative forces of society. That nationalist forces are not as idealistic as we should like, or the influence of the Christian morality as great as we should like, must be admitted. That materialistic influences may yet succeed in getting control of nationalism must also be admitted. The situation is by no means closed, and the struggle is only beginning. Agitation for the thorough moralization of nationalism is at present no longer possible in several countries of Europe, and in other countries the emphasis is on the prevention of war rather than on the Christianizing of the forces that might otherwise make toward war. The situation is serious, but no one who has any regard for the world in which our descendants must live, and who feels any responsibility for making that world better than that of the present, can shrink from the effort to give moral direction to political forces. We cannot expect immediate success, but every citizen who really believes that it is possible to establish an international morality will not abandon intelligent effort to give politics moral direction. For the choice is not between the political issues of the past. Today the world faces the choice between a morality of nations and revolution, war, chaos, and misery.

VIII

There remains the perplexing question; is it permissible to believe that national groups are capable of intelligent self-direction? The conventionally Protestant religious reply would probably be in the affirmative. Certainly the liberals of the nineteenth century would have made the same

Christianity and Internationalism

reply. To them democracy and self-government were synonymous with national happiness. In economics *laissez-faire* and unrestrained competition were to be the guarantees of prosperity. In politics that government was best which governed least.

It would be supererogatory to argue that among nations where these philosophies have been actually tried there is a growing distrust of their efficiency. Life has grown so complicated, the relation of groups involves so many interests, and the material wealth involved in any readjustment is so enormous that great masses of people seem incompetent to face actual situations as they arise. The appeal of leaders, both in industry and in politics, is to prejudice and passion quite as commonly as in days when the issues at stake were far less complicated. Too often national enmities are transferred to an adopted country. Even more frequently the actions of a representative government are brought to a deadlock by virtue of unwillingness of different sections or different interests of a country to make concessions in the interests of a national good. Human intelligence

Christianity and Social Process

and human good will have not kept pace with the enormous economic expansion of the last generation. We are attempting to face problems of worldwide extent by the techniques of the tribe or the isolated nation. It is no wonder that nations turn from the endless debates of legislatures that have preferred loquacity to intelligence, and are submitting themselves to control in whose organization they have no real part.

The student of morals looks with apprehension upon this loss of confidence in collective human agency. The substitution of coercion for self-direction is something more than a means of new efficiency. It is a confession of moral incapacity and unintelligence. It may indeed be an indication that human history runs in cycles, that a civilization can be self-administering up to a certain degree of development, but will then collapse because of its incapacity to carry its own weight. This was true of many great civilizations, and has been prophesied with vast erudition for our own day.

It is quite impossible to deny the danger which the present rapid changes throughout the entire

Christianity and Internationalism

world involve. But to observe symptoms is not to diagnose a disease, and even a disease may be a form of ill-directed and excessive life. Indeed, the analogy may be carried out farther. It is not so many years since men undertook to cure diseases by bleeding their patients. Now, having come to see that so many diseases are due to bacteria, much therapeutic effort is directed toward the building up of living organisms which preserve the life of the human organism as a whole. Similarly, a social process can be vitalized with moral idealism and religious faith.

We are confronted with an inescapable decision. Shall we look to the future with hopefulness or with despair? Are we to think because we have dared to be optimistic and have been deceived by those who have exploited us, that our only recourse is defeatism and frustration and revolution? There will be those who are too cowardly or mentally soggy to face such a decision frankly. They will prefer to live as parasites on other people's attitudes. For such persons one can have little respect. But for those of us who feel some

Christianity and Social Process

sense of moral responsibility for the creation of the social mind there can be no such inertness. It may not be better to be a Pollyanna than a Schopenhauer, but there is a still more excellent way. It is that of intelligent optimism born of Christian faith, which, while recognizing the liabilities of human history, also counts its assets. For those who possess that hopefulness the task of directing a social process in such a way that it shall not bring distress becomes imperative. To them history is not to be explained in any single formula, least of all by economic determinism. Christian hopefulness is more than a sentimental anesthetic to deaden participation in the struggle for human betterment. To neglect it or to exploit it is to make pessimism desperate and to offer occasion to those who would substitute the counsel of despair for intelligently directed social evolution. To make it a social ferment is to insure social health. As the Christian movement has given direction to many of the elements of the social process from which Western civilization has developed, so may we trust that it will give the moral qualities of the ideals of its founder and of the values it has

Christianity and Internationalism

embodied to that nationalist civilization which is in the making.

Several conclusions seem inevitable from this survey of the part taken by the Christian religion in the development of Western civilization.

In the first place it seems clear that it has acted as a ferment in social change rather than as the initiator of such changes. The effort of Christians to detach themselves from social relations in the interest of the values which their religion preserved has not furthered moral advance in society as a whole. The Christian movement has not been effective as an escape technique. Its greatest development has been in moments of crisis, when the controls of the past have been outgrown and social change has called for heroic action. In such moments of crisis Christian values have usually been brought to bear on the process of change by those who have broken from the control of ecclesiastical institutions and have organized Christian groups which embodied a new social mind. These groups have been decreasingly ecclesiastical in character. This can be seen in the

Christianity and Social Process

sequence of Roman Catholicism, Protestant state churches, nonconformist churches, Christian associations, charitable and philanthropic institutions, social-service clubs.

This process of differentiation, with its distinction between the values and the doctrines of the Christian movement, has been due in no small measure to the rise of the historical study of the life and teaching of Jesus. The relative character of Christian institutions and doctrines in their perpetuation of anachronistic modes of thought and social organization is now clearly seen. Jesus has become the hero of the depressed classes, and of those socially-minded members of the privileged groups who feel the injustices and inequalities of the present day. Unlike the fraternities of the Middle Ages, those who possess this new appreciation of Jesus do not emphasize the externals of his life like poverty and celibacy, but his teachings and spiritual attitudes. He is less a Christ to be imitated than a founder of a religious movement whose values are to be implemented intelligently as factors in a social process.

The second conclusion is that while the Chris-

Christianity and Internationalism

tian movement, because of its organic connection with a total social process, has been subject to the influences of institutions and practices, it has none the less been consistently opposed to those elements of that process which threaten the supremacy of personal and moral values. The larger social intelligence of our day makes more distinct the opposition of the Christian philosophy of life to those programs of social reconstruction which minimize the importance of the individual and rely upon coercion, if not terror. Unless all signs fail this difference is likely to become increasingly an issue in the present stage of a social process which is no longer limited to Europe and America. The responsibility of the churches is therefore for something more than ecclesiastical prosperity. The social development of the future will be largely determined by their success in educating the groups resulting from and causing social change to stand for personal values and the democratization of privilege into universal rights.

A third conclusion is that this opportunity of the Christian movement will not be met either by insisting upon the separation between religion and

Christianity and Social Process

other aspects of the social life or by the substitution of social programs for its own function. As a part of a social order its chief significance will be the production of individuals and groups capable of giving moral direction to the forces of social reconstruction, and in uncompromising opposition to such forces as would belittle the personal worth of the individual. By participating in and inspiring the social process as it exists today Christians can save the world from distrust of that heritage of hope that sprang from the democratic movement with its new sense of the worth of the individual. Groups and nations now need the same motivation that gave moral significance to individualism. Nothing but disaster can follow the implementing of idealism with violence or treating Christianity as if it were without social obligations. As a phase of Western civilization which is now affecting the entire world, the function of the Christian movement is obvious. As a social behavior, it can impregnate social change with the ideals it has conserved as the contribution of its Founder.

THE END

INDEX

Alexander VI, 137
Ambrose, 153
Anabaptists, 160
Art, influence of church on, 54
Attitudes, relation to techniques, 93

Benedict, 153
Benedict XII and war, 203
Boniface VIII, 204
Buddhism, an aspect of a civilization, 11

Calvinism and capitalism, 163 *sq.*
Capitalism, 161, 164
Celibacy, influence of, 91, 107, 122
Charity, 116, 152, *sq.*
Christian Socialists, 167
Christianity, a religion, 3; an aspect of Western civilization, 33; a social movement, 34; its relation with historical forces, 42-49; not to be identified with Western civilization, 43; relation to reforms, 52; as a ferment, 52, 88, 108, 113; values it conserves, 59 *sq.*; its moral idealism, 84; no caste, 110; and economic evolution, 150; not communistic, 152; and war, 181 *sq.*
Chrysostom, 153
Church, relations with social groups, 46; representative of a *status quo*, 51; conserver of classical culture, 53; and war, 136; and usury, 155; and feudalism, 180; wealth of mediaeval, 156
Churches, state, 162
Clement of Alexandria, 154
Codes, influence of, 85
Coercion, 134
Common law, parallelism with Christianity, 60
Confession, 86 *sq.*
"Copec," 172
Crusades, 136, 203

Declaration of the Rights of Man, 115
Democracy, origin of, 113 *sq.*
Doctrines, means of integrating the Christian movement, 37 *sq.*; origin in social patterns, 61

Index

Elizabeth of England, 137
Excommunication, 136

Federal Council of the Churches of Christ in America, 172
Freedom of conscience, 115

God, growth of the idea of, 17 *sq.*; as love, 68 *sq.*
Gods, prescribe behavior, 11
Grotius, Hugo, 205
Group, morality of, 130 *sq.*

Henry VIII of England, 157
Heresy, 79
Hinduism, an aspect of a civilization, 11
Holy Roman Empire, 53

Immortality and morality, 101
Individuals, Christianity and, 111 *sq.*
Innocent III, 112

Jesus, central in Christianity, 34 *sq.*; social teachings of, 171
Judaism, an aspect of a civilization, 11
"Just price," 158

Latin Christianity, 43
Love, cosmic parallels, 72
Luther and politics, 119; and peasants, 162; and religious liberty, 111

Machines, 166 *sq.*

Marriage, church and, 120
Mary, mother of Jesus, 75
Messianic hope, the, nature of, 35
Methodist movement, 200
Moore, Sir Thomas, 205
Morals and social changes, 24 *sq.*

Nationalism 181, *sq.*; religion and, 186

Old Testament, influence of, 80-83

Papacy, power of, 136
Peasants, revolt of, 162
Persecution, 138, 141
Philip II of Spain, 137
Protestantism, aspects of, 49; and persecution, 139; and democracy, 113; State churches, 162
Psalms of Solomon, 12
Puritanism, influence of, 87

Religion, origin of, 4; and philosophy, 14; and morality, 21, 24, 127
Religions as forms of social behavior, 4 *sq.*; aspects of civilizations, 6 *sq.*; changes in, 20; conservativism of, 27
Revolution, Christianity and, 200
Roman Church, influence of, 78
Russia, church in, 114

Index

Slaves. Christianity and, 52
Social Creed of the Churches, 172
Social gospel, 168, 172
Social process, 5 sq.
Suarez, 205

Thomas Aquinas, 138
"Truce of God," 204

Universal Conference on Christian Life and Work, 172

Universities founded by Church, 54
Usury denounced by church, 155-161

Vittoria, Franciscus di, 205

War, Christianity and, 136, 190 sq.; 203 sq.
Williams, Roger, 115
Woman, status of, 120 sq.

---

3 – 5 – 7 – 15 – 40 – 63 – 64 – 65 – 66 – 67 – 113 – 118 – 126 – 130 – 131 – 169 – 215 – 217.

Christianity and Social Process by Shailer Mathews Harper and Brothers. 229 pages. $2.00

This volume contains the Barrows Lectures of the University of Chicago, for 1933-34, which Dean-Emeritus Mathews gave particularly in India, and also in other parts of the Orient last winter. The material in the book is expanded somewhat from the actual lectures given.

[221]

Dr. Mathews went to India as one who has a very different viewpoint in the interpretation of religion from that of the average Indian Oriental. The philoso-

approach in dealing with religion is native to the Indian. Dean Mathews uses the historical method and the socio-psychological approach. For him, religion does not exist in the abstract. It is a form of social behaviour and Christianity is an aspect of Western Civilization. Every religion is an aspect of some social process and it possesses social control through prescribed social customs far more than through its philosophy.

The titles of the lectures are "Religion and Social Behaviour", "Christianity as an aspect of Western Civilization", "The Moral Nature of the Christian Religion", "Christianity and the Individual", "Christianity and the Morality of Groups", "Christianity and Economics", and "Christianity and Internationalism".

Dr. Mathews' conclusions as to the part played by Christianity in the development of Western Civilization are sane and thoughtful. Christianity is a ferment in social change rather than the initiator of such changes. Even though it has an organic connection with Western social life it has always been consistently opposed to the elements of that process which threaten the supremacy of personal and moral values. Christianity cannot perform its mission either by insisting upon the separation between religion and other aspects of the social life or by substituting social progress for its own function. It must act as leaven.

This work is the third in a trilogy of which the other two are <u>The Atonement and the Social Process</u>, and <u>The Growth of the Idea of God</u>.